Helen Gordon:
The Woman behind the *Greensheet*

A Daughter's Memoir of Helen Gordon, Founder of the *Greensheet*

REBECCA BLAKELEY

iUniverse, Inc.
Bloomington

HELEN GORDON: THE WOMAN BEHIND THE GREENSHEET

iUniverse books may be ordered through booksellers or by contacting:

iUniverse
1663 Liberty Drive
Bloomington, IN 47403
www.iuniverse.com
1-800-Authors (1-800-288-4677)

Because of the dynamic nature of the Internet, any web addresses or links contained in this book may have changed since publication and may no longer be valid. The views expressed in this work are solely those of the author and do not necessarily reflect the views of the publisher, and the publisher hereby disclaims any responsibility for them.

Any people depicted in stock imagery provided by Thinkstock are models, and such images are being used for illustrative purposes only.

Certain stock imagery © Thinkstock.

ISBN: 978-1-4759-8706-5 (sc)
ISBN: 978-1-4759-8705-8 (hc)
ISBN: 978-1-4759-8704-1 (e)

Library of Congress Control Number: 2013907266

Printed in the United States of America.

iUniverse rev. date: 5/20/2013

This book is dedicated in loving memory to
my mother,
Helen Gordon,
1928–2010.

Acknowledgments

With Dr. Rev. Morledge's and Barbara Harding's urging, I began to write with a goal to finish this book about my mother. I want to thank Dr. Rev. Morledge, Barbara Harding, Bill Chaney, Ted Stiles, Mike Stermon Jr., Mike Bergdahl, Brian De Young, Bob De Young, and Kathy Douglass for the stories they have given me to complete Mother's story. A special thanks to my friend Cindy Golden, who continually inspired me. In addition, to my editor, Genevieve Fosa, for helping me give these stories life.

Table of Contents

Introduction

ELEN GORDON ALWAYS HAD A vision to run her own business. In 1970, she started the *Greensheet,* a free advertising tabloid with classified ads for sale and business services to serve local areas of Houston, Dallas, Fort Worth, and Austin. A tough female entrepreneur who faced incredible resistance from the good ol' boy atmosphere, she demonstrated great resolve in getting the *Greensheet* off the ground and turned the company into a powerhouse.

As a family we worked and helped my mother build a healthy company. The publication remains a family-owned business by her two daughters, Kathy Douglass and Rebecca Blakeley. My sister, Kathy, is the current publisher and CEO, and I have remained on the board of directors. While working with my mother with two of her companies in a span of twenty-nine years, our relationship was always a close one.

My mother was not the kind of person who spent much time reflecting on the past. She was too involved in the present, building her business, spending time with her second husband, Bob, and with her devoted family. Wanting to know and share with others about this amazing woman who raised us, guided us, and inspired us to become who we are today, in the summer of 2009, I persuaded Mother to let me help her write her memoirs. Throughout those coming months, we had wonderful conversations about her early childhood, her years as a working mother, and anything else she felt like sharing. As usual, she was completely honest about herself, blunt and to the point. My mother was a kind, complicated woman who forged her own path when few women of her day dared to—a wonderful wife and mother who set the example for her children of having a strong work ethic and a woman who never shied away from speaking truthfully, no matter what the cost.

When Mother and Robert De Young married in 1969, they thought of three different cities—Denver, Atlanta, and Houston. Bob thought Mother would like Houston due to the economic climate of the city; the people were flexible, and it could be a healthy city for new business. After moving to Houston, Helen took a vacation. During that vacation she thought of what business she would like to open. The decision to start an advertising publication was one of three choices. Having experience in all three, she thought of an art gallery, an ad agency, or an advertising paper. The last one would combine all her experience into one. Mother was determined to own and operate her own company. Her reason was to be her own boss, and Mother believed that the ideas she had for running her own company would be successful. By March 1970 she delivered the first *Greensheet* to grocery stores, 7-Elevens, and a variety of local stores in the southwest area of Houston. By the time Mother retired she had grown the company to one of the most successful classified tabloids in the state. My mother died of lung cancer March 31, 2010, and was not able to see this memoir completed. This is the story of her life and how she pioneered her way into business.

Nickels in a Jar

MY MOTHER, HELEN LOUISE GORDON, born December 19, 1928, spent her early childhood in the midst of the Great Depression. Her father had the foresight to move out to the country, where they could keep a garden, so her family was perhaps better off than many other families of that time. The garden kept most of the food on the table, as there were the vegetables and fruits my grandmother canned. Meat was a rarity they could only afford a few times a week. They used canned milk and had no condiments such as ketchup, mustard, or butter. My grandparents, William John and Rebecca Grace Gordon, both expected to work and were proud to do what they could. Grandfather worked as a master carpenter and my grandmother was a nurse.

Grandmother was named for her mother, Rebecca Jane; everyone called my grandmother Grace, as the name fit her so well. As a young woman, she defied cultural norms when she went to nursing school against her father's wishes. This was in 1918, shortly after the Spanish flu epidemic, which followed the First World War. Hundreds of thousands of people died from the Spanish flu, possibly because those people had lived through several years of a very restricted diet, due to the privations of the war. Too many people at that time had no resistance to the flu. The only things they knew to do against contagious illnesses was to quarantine infected people, in order to try prevent it from spreading, and drink wine or other alcohol four times a day. Alcohol was known to be a disinfectant, and the hope was that disease-causing agents would not be able to survive in a body that was well hydrated with the stuff.

Today some people prefer to drink milk that has not been pasteurized, as it contains proteins that are killed during the pasteurization process. People forget that milk fresh from the cow may also contain other elements and bacteria that can be harmful to us. In the early 1900s, most milk was not heat treated before it was sold, as few people thought it was necessary. My grandmother contracted a terrible infection, diphtheria, after drinking such milk. She was sick with this for weeks, and the illness left a scar on her face that forever embarrassed her, even after a surgeon had removed as much of it as he could when she was a young woman. Grace admired the doctor, who operated on her for what he was able to do, and she then decided she would like to study medicine, perhaps to become a doctor. She began by enrolling in nursing school. Her sister Mary, not to be outdone, decided she would go to nursing school as well. It would be a lot more fun than sitting at home, waiting for a suitor to sweep her off her feet. Besides, if the sisters went together, they could keep each other company and help each other over the tough places.

I can only imagine the arguments my great-grandfather Moses Fulton Douglass must have had with both his daughters for doing this scandalous thing. The girls could wind up being a disgrace to the entire family. My grandmother stood her ground, and her father finally relented and allowed them to go to nursing school.

In those days, nursing was not one of the most respectable professions for a woman to have. The work was dirty, and young women could be exposed to all sorts of crudities, not to mention illnesses. The world had not yet learned of antibiotics, so the known remedy was to quarantine to protect other people from the illnesses, which was often life threatening. Liquor was often used medicinally, as well as herbs and prayers, and sometimes those remedies worked. The administrators of those schools did everything they could to maintain propriety. The young women had to live at the school, dress modestly, keep a strict curfew, and avoid going out on dates.

Grace wanted still to be a doctor. Until the day she got married, she had entertained hopes of somehow getting into medical school.

However, medical schools were expensive. The competition was tough and exacting, and it was even harder for a woman. If being a nurse was stepping beyond the limits imposed upon the women of my grandmother's generation, entering medical school and studying to be a doctor would have been too horrifying for most good people to tolerate. It was expected that any job would end the day a woman got married. From there she would stay at home, working to maintain a sense of cultural enlightenment within her family and taking care of her children. Higher education was essentially wasted on a woman, or so many people said. It was considered the wife's job to bring art and music into the home, to subdue her husband's more violent character traits, and to keep morals within the household supremely high. Working as a nurse, a woman would get to see a man's naked body, and she might have to do things to it that were most unseemly. Studying to be a doctor would be even worse, as she would be expected to dissect cadavers with young men and jockey for position with them in the classroom.

By the time my grandmother was in her teens, the First World War had started. People then did not call it that, because nobody at that time wanted to believe that there could be another war as horrific. It was known as the Kaiser's war, or the war in Europe. The men went off to fight, leaving the women at home to take care of business. This meant that scores of women had to leave their kitchens in order to go to work. They needed practical clothes to do practical things, so skirts came up off the floor, and corsets, for the most part, disappeared. My grandmother and her sister Mary were part of a generation of strong women who entered the twentieth century with their eyes wide open and their hands ready to do whatever had to be done.

In 1923, Grace graduated from the Shadyside Hospital School of Nursing and began working there as a nurse. She never did go beyond nursing school; she was proud to work as a nurse, proud of the sense of independence this gave her before she was married, and very pleased with the respect she received from her colleagues. By the time she was twenty-five, she had saved enough money to buy herself a home. The home at that time was valued at $10,500, located in Brookline, Pennsylvania. This display of independence ultimately earned her father's respect. However, until she had established herself as a nurse and proven that she could take care of herself, Grace Douglass and her father were very much at odds.

Her sister Mary, while exceptionally intelligent, did not do as well in nursing school. She had to leave after a few months of study. She went back to her father's home and stayed there to take care of him until the day he died. She did find work in a drug store, but she was never truly able to support herself.

My grandmother was a petite woman, standing about five feet one. When I try to describe my grandmother, the words that come to mind are kind, forgiving, and soft spoken. The nurses she worked with called her Gentle Cousin. Grace was a devout Christian who believed everything in the Bible. However, unlike some fundamentalist Christians, she was not small minded. She understood that everyone sees the world based on their own experiences and that people from different places and cultures may have vastly different expectations concerning what the world holds for them.

The man who would be her husband, Bill Gordon, had been working since he was thirteen years old at a carpentry mill. My family says that he had to stand on a bench in order to reach his assigned tasks. He was one of those young men who learned early in life the meaning of work and being self-sufficient. My grandfather's father was also a strict disciplinarian, and my grandfather left home early because of the turmoil.

In 1910, when my grandfather turned seventeen, he enlisted in the navy just in time for World War I. He served for eight years and seven months in the navy, earning the rank of chief petty officer before his discharge. He had lied about his age in order to be admitted. At the time he enlisted he was perhaps looking for adventure. He did manage to travel all over the world and sadly contracted malaria, a disease that never really leaves its victims. By 1914, he was in the midst of fighting the Great War.

When he did return home, in 1920, he had no desire to make

the armed forces his career. He believed he had served his time and that he had risked his life for his country as much as any man should be expected to. He settled down to marry a young woman by the name of Margaret Fricke. Margaret gave birth to one child, who died within a year, and then, in 1922, she herself died while attempting to give birth to a second child. William Gordon deeply mourned his wife's death. Still, he must have been at least a little willing to consider the possibility of marrying again, for his sister, Great Aunt Betty, who worked as a nurse with Grace, told Grace, "I'd like you to meet my brother." Gentle and strong minded, Grace Douglass appealed to Bill Gordon, for on September 25, 1926, William J. Gordon married my grandmother. For the first couple of years they lived together in the house she had bought. However, the Depression was affecting everyone. Jobs were scarce, and people who had jobs did not know how long they would be able to keep them. After living in the country a few years, they decided to move to be closer to the hospitals so that Grandmother could find work, so they moved to 555 Orchard Avenue in Bellevue, Pennsylvania, a suburb of Pittsburgh. There, my mother, Helen Gordon, was born on December 19, 1928. Two years later my uncle Dan was born, on September 30, 1930.

We cannot know how the death of his first wife, Margaret, affected his relationship with his second wife and their two children. Who knows whether he cherished his children more because he had lost two other children or because he was inclined to hold his emotions back and not be as free with his affections as he might have, for fear of being hurt again. As an adult, our mother did not easily show affection and did not tolerate emotional displays from her children. Had she learned this from her father? Margaret Fricke always held a special place in my grandfather's heart, and he frequently spoke of her as being perfect in ways that no one could surpass. I don't believe my grandmother was ever jealous or upset over the way he spoke of his first wife. If she was, she quickly learned to take his reminiscing with a grain of salt. "After all," she told me years later, "Margaret is dead and Bill is with me."

I still have a set of bone china that Margaret painted by hand.

Very neatly and carefully, she painted a border of green leaves entwined with yellow and pink roses around each cup and plate and serving dish. There must have been at least sixty pieces in the set originally. My grandmother and my mother both cherished this china, before passing it on to me.

Bill Gordon really did love Grace. She was always a little bit overweight, but Bill used to say, "I like a woman with a little meat on her bones." My grandmother would blush and say, "Oh, Bill."

Their children, Helen and Dan, both felt protected by their parents. Years later, my mother told me that when she was growing up she felt that if her father had been elected president, he could have solved all the world's problems. At any rate, Bill said he knew everything, and when my mother was a child, she believed him. He was strict with his children. He established the rules, which my mother and her brother knew they must follow. Grandfather had come out of an era that had much less patience with children than we do now. His children were only to be seen, never to be heard. That was also a phrase that we were taught by when we were in the company of adults. Being respectful to their father meant keeping their conversations away from him, as well as being clean and dutiful at all times.

My mother modified his rules when I was growing up. She believed that children should be permitted, even encouraged, to speak their minds, but that they must do so with respect for their elders. I must have been about eight or nine years old when I asked her, "But how do you know when I'm not respectful?"

"Because I know you."

And later, when I was upset about something that had gone wrong, she said, "You can't get into any kind of trouble that I haven't already." If I had been a little older when she said this, I might have asked her what sort of trouble she had got into when she was growing up, as I would have treasured those stories. Mother wasn't the sort of person to volunteer that sort of information. She strongly believed that we need to live in the present and work for the future. The past is gone and done, and nothing can change it.

My grandmother was an intelligent and hard-working woman who was frugal in ways that most people would not even consider. For example, she used to patch her shoes when the soles wore through. This is something most of us would not know how to do. She taught my mother how to knit and sew, not because she thought they were nice things to do but because she thought them necessary. Money might not always be available, so one must know how to clothe one's family. Doing for yourself, making what you needed, and making do with what you had were ideals that became second nature to many people who lived through the Great Depression.

Even with all her frugal homemaker skills, my grandmother did not derive pleasure from cooking. As long as she put enough nourishing food in front of the family, she felt she could be done with it. Every morning before school, she would serve her children a platter of buckwheat pancakes. My mother hated them. Oatmeal? Scrambled eggs? Fruit in season? All these things would have been a welcome change. However, it was unfailingly buckwheat pancakes with syrup for breakfast.

Mother did make pancakes for us when I was growing up, but never buckwheat. After she left her parents' home, she decided she liked Cream of Wheat cereal. I hate to think of those bowls of hot Cream of Wheat I sat in front of, desultorily pushing the spoon through the lumps as the cereal slowly cooled. I used to add as much sugar as I could to the stuff just to make it taste like something. However, my older sister Kathy loved to eat it, encouraging our mother to keep on fixing it for our breakfast.

When my sister, brother, and I were little, we were expected to dress in clean, neat clothes before we sat down to eat our dinner. My mother also insisted that paper plates were not meant for indoor use, so even when we had friends over and we knew there would be a lot of dishes to wash, we did not use paper plates.

Ideas about the duties women should have and the roles they should play were changing, both at home and in the workplace. In 1918, women over the age of thirty were conceded the right to vote, because the men were fighting the Great War in Europe. By 1920, women from the age of eighteen and up could vote, just as men did. Grace saw how women had to fight for their rights and believed the right to value and control her own life was perhaps the best thing she could teach her daughter. Helen and her brother Dan grew up expecting that women could and should be independent and know how to carry responsibility just as well as men could.

As long as the school was within a mile to a mile and a half of where the children lived, they were expected to walk to and from school every day. Most of these children walked home for lunch in the middle of the day and then walked back to school for the afternoon session. For some children it meant hiking to and from school at least four miles every day.

In the afternoon, my mother and my uncle Dan would walk home for lunch. Often, Dan would stop at the store on the way home to pick up some cold cuts so they could have sandwiches for their lunch. Grace worked at the hospital at night and slept when her children were at school, but she was always up in the middle of the day when her children came home for lunch, with stories about what had been going on at the hospital where she worked. Her stories were nearly always touching and often funny, and they may have been more important to her children than the sandwiches she served them for their noon meal.

Helen's father was firmly rooted within the Victorian consciousness instilled in him when he was growing up. He believed he should make sure any daughter of his would learn how to play a musical instrument as well as the housewifely arts of sewing and cooking. My mother learned how to bake a lemon pie when she was seven years old, an experience that she always remembered with pride. Her mother had put a great big apron on her, helped her sort out the ingredients, and then read the recipe to her while Helen mixed and stirred to the best of her ability. Everyone must have pronounced it an excellent pie, as my mother always enjoyed experimenting with recipes and making nice dinners for her family and friends. Her father also made sure that his daughter had piano lessons. My mother didn't like to practice playing. Very few young children do enjoy the discipline of daily practice, especially when they must repeat the same uninspiring lines of music. Through those first few years, Grace would sit down beside her when she practiced, encouraging her when the going was difficult and praising her when she played something especially well.

There was one song Mother had to play for her instructor, called "Twinkle Toes." It was one of those horrible little ditties that nearly every beginning piano student must learn to play. Uncle Dan hated it. Every time my mother had to practice it, he would pitch his shoes down the stairs at her. It didn't take Mother long to realize that in her hands lay a weapon far more potent than the shoes her brother threw at her. Mother would retaliate by playing louder. Dan could pitch more shoes at her, but he could not force her to stop practicing; after all, their parents were paying for those lessons. Uncle Dan cherished the lessons his father gave him about working with wood. He always loved to work with his hands and later became a master carpenter, as was my grandfather.

Dinner was always served at five in the evening, when Bill came home from work. Every evening the family would put on clean, neat clothes before sitting down to eat. My grandfather would come downstairs wearing a clean shirt and tie, no matter how warm the weather was, and he expected that his wife and children to show the same respect.

My grandfather was as strict with his wife as he was with his children. When she cooked, he expected her to add all the salt the food would need while it was still on the stove. He did not want to have to add any more at the table. Even less did he want his children to mess around with salt. If the food was not salted to suit his taste, he vehemently let Grace know how he felt so that she would not make that mistake again. This may have been at least part of the reason why my grandmother seldom felt inspired to do any creative cooking. She and her husband often had terrible arguments over her housekeeping; one thing out of place and he would point it out, sometimes with anger. Any woman who works outside the home knows how difficult it is to find the time to maintain the household and take care of the children. With these disagreements aside, Grace and Bill truly enjoyed being together. They loved talking with each other and they looked forward to their evening conversations.

Even though Grace did not care for cooking, she always was an old-fashioned sort of housekeeper. She made sure she had some cookies, cinnamon rolls, or at least some fresh baked bread to serve her guests when they came to visit. At Christmastime, she would make caramel turtles or candied orange peels as gifts for her friends. She knitted and crocheted blankets, sewed, and made herself what we today buy at the store. It was part of the culture at that time. Up through the late 1920s and into the 1930s, many people had ice delivered to their homes to keep their food fresh for a few days. Milk would not stay fresh in the icebox for more than a day or two, and jugs of milk take up precious food storage space when you are feeding a large family. Helen's mother used canned milk in her cooking and served it to her children to drink. My mother couldn't stand it and stopped drinking canned milk as soon as she was permitted to do so. The coolants used in those early refrigerators were said to be unsafe to keep in one's home. Besides, refrigerators were expensive, and my grandfather, a frugal man, would not have wanted to spend his money unnecessarily. They continued to use their icebox into the late 1940s, when my brother was born.

For Helen and her brother, perhaps more difficult than his frugality was the expectation that children should be silent after supper so that their parents could converse with each other in peace. As they grew older, it is easy to imagine the two of them going to their rooms where they could play a quiet game, or read, or study until it was time for bed. But as toddlers and very young children, this must have been most difficult for them, as well as their mother, who did not want to be cruel to her children, but did need them to be quiet.

My family is so busy that I feel a sense of triumph when we all manage to sit down to a meal at the same time. However, in my grandmother's home, they showed respect for each other and appreciation for the food they were eating in this formal way, even if my grandmother's meals were simple and repetitive. There is something to be said for taking some time out of each day to concentrate on being sweet and respectful toward the other members of the family.

Grace must have had the patience of a saint. When she was little, my mother insisted that all the sheets she slept on be ironed. She could always tell when they hadn't been and never hesitated to let her mother know when her bed sheets did not meet her standards. My grandmother used to iron those sheets without a word of protest. She did the family laundry in a wringer washer and hung it up to dry. She expected to have to iron nearly everything before it could be used, even though her time was limited. Grace did not iron sheets for anyone else in the house, just her little girl. Neither her husband nor her son insisted they sleep on this sort of luxury, but as long as her daughter wanted ironed sheets, she would give them to her.

My grandmother was born in 1900. As a young couple during the 1930s, she and her husband bought themselves a wringer washer, which was state of the art for that time and a wonderfully timesaving device. No longer did a woman have to stand in front of a wash tub, scrubbing heavy towels and work clothes out by hand. My grandfather was young and he believed his wife should have nothing but the best. It had to be good, because it must last for years. I believe my grandmother was still using that ringer washing machine up into the 1960s. *Waste not want not* was a creed to live by, not simply a pretty aphorism. Her husband spent about thirty dollars on that machine. It doesn't sound like a lot of money now, until you look at that sum in relation to inflation. In today's money that would be nearly four hundred. For my grandfather at the time, it might as well have been four thousand dollars. It is no wonder my grandmother continued to use that wringer washer for so long.

Most of us grew up in what we call a nuclear family. The notion of adult relatives sharing a dwelling is something that we as a society are just beginning to reconsider, as our economy worsens. The household Helen grew up in would have been culturally less rich and perhaps a little less loving had her aunt Mary Douglass not been there. She was a tall, good looking young woman, and there were men interested in courting her, but she was not interested in any of them, so she stayed home to take care of her father. She used to say, "I just never met a man I wanted to keep." When her father died in 1936 at the age of seventy-three, Grace and Bill opened their home to her and she lived with them until her death. Helen was eight years old and Dan was six in September of that year.

Aunt Mary proved to be a storehouse of information. She had a reputation for being able to answer questions and explain nearly everything. How does a combustion engine work? What do we see reflected when the sky looks blue to us? She would read stories to the children, making them feel as though they were at a play put on just for them. She could recite poetry and explain history. It is a truism that extremely intelligent people often need to be taken care of. Much of the time their minds are directed somewhere else rather than on those mundane needs such as clothes, food, and shelter, which occupy the rest of us. The day-to-day trivia of getting themselves to work on time and making sure they are prepared to do the job they were hired to do and do it well is peripheral rather than central to their thinking. *It's raining out. I wonder whether I need to wear my boots or take my umbrella. I'd better ask to make sure.* That was how Aunt Mary was. However, Aunt Mary helped take care of Helen and Dan while they were growing up, and in return, the Gordons took care of her. As a result, Helen and Dan grew up with a sense of love and compassion that otherwise would not have been so well planted in their characters.

To join the Daughters of American Revolution, Great Aunt Mary did tedious library work, wrote letters, and found William Barnes, our ancestral grandfather, as a Revolutionary War Veteran. The process took years, and in 1945, Great Aunt Mary, Grandmother, and later my mother became members of the DAR. William Barnes was traced back through the Fulton family from Westmoreland County, Pennsylvania. My mother, my grandmother, and Great Aunt Mary were proud to be able to join the DAR. Myself and my cousins were able to join due to Great Aunt Mary's work.

Mother has said that Great Aunt Mary and Grandfather seldom appeared to get along. Perhaps this was because Grandfather felt overwhelmed in a household with two strong-minded women. Aunt Mary was quite capable of holding her own in an argument, when she chose to. Neither my grandmother nor Great Aunt Mary would have hesitated to question my grandfather's authority if they believed for even a moment that he was likely to jeopardize what they considered necessary or important. Still, Great Aunt Mary was living in that household at Grandfather's sufferance, and he may have felt called upon to keep her in her place. When she died, April 9, 1965, my grandfather was heard to say, "People don't know, but I did love your aunt Mary."

My mother was about eighteen months older than Uncle Dan, and while they were growing up, she was naturally the responsible one of those two, at least where money was concerned. She insisted on being meticulous with any money that she earned, and she loved earning money. When she was a little girl, her father would pay her a nickel every time she washed his car. As a result, he had a very clean car. At the age of five, she announced to her mother that she was going to be a millionaire when she grew up. Even then she could see that the independence money could give was special, and she was determined to gain it. However, it was not long before she realized that washing the car, or any other chores she could find that her parents might pay her to do, would never earn the kind of money she wanted. She refused to let all her money be spent on little things that would soon be gone. Dan was more impetuous. The little pleasures of today meant a whole lot to him than a few nickels hoarded in a jar until there were enough to get something big. With Great Aunt Mary's influence, the two of them learned to compromise and to respect and care for each other. It was a tough battle. Helen and Dan were strong-minded children. The family used to say that they had the fighting spirit of the Douglass clan, or the Gordon clan, depending on which relative was talking. They each knew that he (or she) was the only one who could ever be right in an argument, and the other one was absolutely wrong. They had more fistfights than anyone would care to count.

Aunt Mary, who loved them both dearly and wouldn't have dared to raise a hand against either of them, was driven to her wits' end. "If you don't stop this right now, I'm going to get the bears from the woods to eat you up!" My uncle Danny must have been about five or six years old when he dashed to the front door, opened it, and called out, "Bears, bears! Come on in and get Aunt Mary."

As they grew, they would go to the movies together, taking turns so they could each have something they wanted. One week Dan would invite a few of his friends to accompany them, and they would see a movie he had chosen. The following week, Helen would invite two or three of her friends to go with them, and they would see a movie she had picked. By the time they were in high school, they had worked out most of their differences. On weekends, they would walk into town together, sometimes with his friends and sometimes with hers, but always enjoying each other's company.

Bill Gordon said his son was supposed to learn how to build things. He taught my uncle Dan how to work with wood. Dan always treasured those times he and his father shared, building things together, and he became a skillful carpenter.

Dan started working with his father in the carpentry mill almost before he had graduated from high school, just as his father had worked at the foundry years before. He always derived a great deal of pleasure out of working with his hands. He earned his living with this work for many years.

In 1948, when Dan was seventeen years old, he enlisted in the navy. He was just the age his father had been when he joined. The war to end all wars had not ended much of anything. Dan was too young to fight in the Second World War, but he did enlist in time to fight in Korea. At that time, he was a machinist mate on the carrier USS *Hornet*. His experiences there aged him. Seeing his buddies injured and killed, while having to participate in killing other young soldiers, tore at his heart. When he returned, the easy friendships he had enjoyed before joining the navy were nearly a thing of the past. He married soon after his return to the States, in 1953, and he concentrated on his work and making a home for Mabel, his new wife. However, no matter how heartsick and withdrawn he felt, he maintained his affection for his sister Helen.

Dan's wife, Mabel was the daughter of Granpap's best friend, and Dan had known her for years. Mabel had grown up on a farm in a home that must have been at least as strict as my grandfather William Gordon had made his home. For a combination of reasons, my uncle Dan chose to be the same sort of disciplinarian his father had been before him. I have often wondered at the contrast between Uncle Dan's home and my mother's. He believed strongly in the dictum he had grown up with: children are to be seen and not heard.

As a young girl, my mother was an exceptional student. When she was eleven years old, she was surprised to discover that she had a knack for drawing anything she wanted to. She used to entertain herself and her friends in study hall by drawing pictures of them. They were simple pencil sketches on tablet paper, and she seldom had to spend more than a few moments with any one picture. Her friends would pester her for pictures of themselves. She told me that one evening she came home from school and drew a picture of her father seated in his rocking chair, reading the paper. "Every night he used to come home and read the paper, and he sat so still." When she was finished, she found that the sketch she had drawn of his face was, in her words, "just like him."

My grandparents must have been very impressed, because soon after this they sent my mother to the Carnegie Mellon Art Institute. There she learned how to use oils and pastels, and she studied many of the technical aspects of composition and perspective. By the time she entered high school, she was an accomplished artist, able to draw things that her art teachers could not.

"Oh," she told me, "they knew how to teach, but they didn't know anything about art." Her art teachers had her demonstrate various techniques to her classmates. And, of course, there were always posters to be drawn for dances and other events, and my mother made a lot of them. She told me there were only three or four other students at her school who could draw as well as she did.

The responsibilities Helen learned to carry at school ultimately gave her a sense of control over her life. This must at times have left her parents feeling breathless, although my mother did try to be careful to keep her escapades away from their eyes and ears. My grandfather did not believe that a young woman should go out riding in a car with a young man. After all, he had been young once, and he knew how the close confines of a car could lead to things no daughter of his should even think about until the day she was married. He also said that my mother should not go ice skating in public rinks. This was an unladylike activity, and she might be caught in a compromising position should she fall down on the ice. No, absolutely not. She was not to go skating at a public rink or ride in a car with a young man, not as long as she lived under his roof. Mother managed to find ways to do those things anyway.

I believe that for my mother the word *no* posed a challenge, a roadblock put in her way to be climbed over, around, or tunneled through. This is obviously the spirit that helped her to rise in her business life.

Move to the Country

MY PARENTS MET WHEN SHE was thirteen and he was seventeen. He was about average height and so fair, with white-blond hair, that people called him Whitey. He was a drummer in his own band, playing jazz and swing, and the kids called it Whitey's Band. His real name was Laverne Gebauer. Mother used to visit him at his home, and he would pound away on his drums while she played the piano. The teenagers in the neighborhood would come out in the street to dance to their music.

Helen and Verne saw each other for much of that first summer of 1942, until he joined the navy and served on the USS *Mississippi* for the next four years. While he was away, she wrote letters to him about once a week, but she really didn't feel excited about him. Waiting for Verne's letters was definitely not as exciting as going out with Joe Kelley, who was just her age. As far as our mother was concerned, Joe was *special special*. He used to park his car down the road from her parents' home, as Mother was not allowed to ride with boys in a car. Then he would walk over with one of his friends, and the three of them would go riding in his car and talk. They loved to talk. Youngsters were more innocent then than they are now. All they did was talk. She and Joe also went ice skating at public rinks together, which was also not allowed. If our grandmother knew about those escapades, she was inclined to say, "Well, we just won't tell your father." Mother's curfew was 11:00 p.m., and Grandpap would be waiting up for her, watching the clock. Anytime she was home one minute passed eleven, strong arguments would arise. When Uncle Dan knew about our mother's ruses to get out of the house, he never gave her secrets away. Helen and Joe saw each other regularly for the next four years.

Meanwhile, Verne sent his navy ring home to Helen. She thought it was interesting, but it really didn't excite her. Being with Joe Kelley was more fun than writing letters to Verne, who had been away all through her high school years. Four years is a long time for a young teenager. Then Verne came home, and Joe was truly upset that she was seeing this older man in the navy. Joe broke up with her, and Verne gave Helen an official diamond engagement ring. Years later, my mother said that she had found that ring to be *very interesting*.

Once she graduated from high school, Helen found a job working at Sears, and she and Verne were soon married and she became Mrs. Laverne Gebauer, August 17, 1945. She was only seventeen at the time, and Verne was twenty-one. Many parents now would say that Helen had not been old enough to know her own mind. If her parents had any qualms about their daughter marrying so young, they didn't express them to her. Besides, Verne appeared to be a steady young man, who would in all probability be a good husband to their daughter and father to their grandchildren. He had joined the navy and done well there, just as her father and brother had. And he liked to work with his hands, just as they did. Some of his ideas may have been different from theirs, but we are not little buttons in a row, and everyone must have felt that Verne would be a good, stable addition to the family. My grandparents, Rose and Homer Gebauer, helped my parents get an apartment right next door to where they lived. Helen and Verne went there every evening after work for the next six months, to scrub the layers of wallpaper off the walls and paint the little rooms so that they would be livable. My mother said that they did not rent a steamer but rather soaked the layers of wallpaper off with hot water, sponges, and solvents.

When she and Verne had finally fixed up the apartment, it didn't look too bad inside. It was part of a row house. It consisted of a block of one- and two-story apartments, lined up down the street. Each apartment had a separate entrance and each room inside the apartment lined up behind the one in front of it, like cars on a train, so that each house would take less space going down the block. The apartment my parents lived in may have been built during the early part of the nineteenth century. The light was blocked from most of the rooms by the house units built on each side, so walking into those little rooms must have felt like walking into a cave, no matter how brightly they were painted. Their apartment didn't have any indoor plumbing, at least no bathroom facilities. The people who owned the house had installed a flush toilet in a shed outside the door. Helen and Verne had to go downstairs and outside to use it, and they had to go to his mother's home when they wanted to take a real bath. Otherwise, they sponged off with a pitcher of water and a bowl in their bedroom, much as their grandparents had done years before.

They lived together this way for a little over a year, and because they were both energetic and very much in love, they did not consider these problems to be hardships. Years later, my mother said that she and our dad had shared a delightful little marriage.

At first, it felt more like playing house than establishing a family, as far as my mother was concerned. Dad was more than happy to have his wife stay at home while he went to work. However, cleaning up their little apartment didn't fill that empty space in my mother's heart and mind. She needed to feel important to the world beyond those four little walls that enclosed their home. First she wanted to have children. She became heartsick that she had not yet become pregnant, even though they had been married a short while. She was doing all she could to let a baby happen, and she was beginning to wonder whether something was wrong with either herself or Dad. It would have felt like a calamity to her if there had been. Mercifully, her unrest didn't last long, as she soon became pregnant with their first child.

Being pregnant made living in that little apartment very uncomfortable. Where keeping clean had been fairly easy before her pregnancy, now it felt like a major proposition, or an imposition, depending on how she felt on any particular day. Having to get up to use the bathroom a couple of times a night didn't help either. Helen was tired and more easily upset about things than she had been before. Of course, Rose and Homer Gebauer would miss being near when the baby came, but everyone believed it was important to get Helen into a comfortable space with proper running water before her baby was born. The Gordons made some drastic changes in their home in order to accommodate Mom and Dad. They moved their bedroom down from the second floor to the living room and made the three rooms on the second floor into a small apartment, with a kitchenette and bathroom, so their daughter could be comfortable through the last weeks of her pregnancy and after the baby was born. Aunt Mary kept the bedroom she had been using upstairs on the third floor.

As far as my mother and father were concerned, the three rooms on the second floor felt like their own apartment, as they could keep everything they needed there and maintain a sense of privacy. Besides, the house on Orchard Avenue was in a very convenient location. Our parents could walk to church, and it took only five minutes to walk to the corner store when they needed something. The business section on Main Street wasn't much farther away, and there they had a variety of nice stores to choose from.

Our dad was contented going to work every day at the mill where our grandfather and uncle worked, and he was proud of his impending fatherhood. On May 19, 1948, Lawrence Robert was born. They named him Lawrence because my mother had always liked the name and Robert because my father thought it to be a fine name for a boy.

Helen described taking care of Larry those first few months after his birth as being intensely tiring. Giving her son a bath would take most of the day. First she had to change him and feed him. Then she would prepare his bathwater, and the temperature had to be just so. She used a thermometer to check it, and if it was too hot she would add cold water, and if it was too cold she added more hot. By then, Larry would want to be fed again. She could not take her eyes off her son for even a moment, fearing he might need something. It took my mother awhile to learn how to hold him properly in the bath and support his head so that he would not get hurt or fall out of her arms.

The whole procedure felt very intricate and shaky. By the time she had finished with his bath, her day had gone by and it was time to fix some dinner, as Dad would be coming home soon. She was so tired that it felt good to have her mother and Aunt Mary nearby, although Helen had always valued her independence so much that asking for help went against her nature.

My sister Kathleen Louise was born almost exactly one year later on May 9, 1949. Mother had been reading *Wuthering Heights* at the time, and the heroine of that story made a deep impression on her, although she changed it from Catherine to Kathleen. Louise was Mother's middle name. I always knew my older sister as Kathy.

My mother's family must have felt complete, especially as she and her husband were still living in those three little rooms. For some reason, taking care of Kathy didn't seem to use nearly as much energy as taking care of Larry had. Larry was decidedly hyperactive throughout his grade school years and had likely been a demanding infant as well. Kathleen may have been a less temperamental baby and my mother was certainly more secure in her ability to care for her children. By the time I came along, two years later, on February 8, 1951, she was an old hand at taking care of babies and toddlers and was beginning to get restless. She named me for my grandmother, Rebecca Grace. When I was very little, people called me Baby Beck, and as I grew older, my nickname became Beck, or Becky.

Shortly after I was born, my grandparents moved to a cabin out in Gibsonia, Pennsylvania, on seven acres of land that my grandfather had bought many years before, thinking that it would be a good place to retire. He had enough land that he believed his son and daughter could build their homes there, if they chose. Back when he first bought the land, he built a three-bedroom cabin on it. He always said that he had built it himself, but I cannot imagine that my uncle Dan and my mother did not help him with this. There would have been much lifting, carting, and pounding, and some things on a construction site almost had to be done with two or more pairs of hands.

Bill and Grace used to take their children out there to camp for a few days each summer. Whatever the situation was, it must not have been very pleasant. My mother always said that camping was dreadful. I'm left to imagine discomforts caused by insects, heat, and rain, made intolerable by a patriarch who would brook no complaints. That could be a dreadful combination. But then, camping is often more pleasant in the abstract past tense, when you can romanticize it and laugh over the mishaps, than it is in the much more definite, itchy, insect-infested, rocky, muddy, wet, or cold, or hot present.

The cabin had stood as a rustic get away in the midst of a pretty piece of woodland until 1951, when I was born. This was when Grandpap and Grandma decided that maybe it was time to move on. They would let my mother and father have the house in town, as long as they paid rent on it, while my grandparents moved out to Gibsonia. With Uncle Dan and my father to help, Grandpa remodeled the cabin so that there would be heat in the winter, a kitchen with running water and a refrigerator, and of course a bathroom. Then they moved the inside walls around so that the three small bedrooms became two larger ones.

Great Aunt Mary stayed in town with us for another year or two. After my grandparents moved to Gibsonia, my mother and father continued to live in Bellevue until I was about four years old. Once Grandma and Grandpap were settled into their home, Grandpap would take Larry or Kathy out there for the weekend, and when I got to be a little older I had my turn as well. Those times were always special. I had my grandmother and grandfather's attention all to myself. I could wander in the woods, play whatever make-believe games I felt like playing, and most importantly, my older brother was not there to tease me. When the weekend was over, Grandpap would bring me back. My parents stayed in Bellevue for about seven years, long enough for Larry to go to first and second grade and Kathy to go to first grade. The houses in town were pretty close together, and many of the families had children our age.

Our mother knew most of the neighbors in Bellevue from when she was a child. She taught Kathy to make fudge and sell it to the neighbors, and she showed both Kathy and Larry how to set up a lemonade stand, where they sold lemonade and perhaps other homemade treats. Any money they earned doing this was saved in a jar so they could buy candy and popsicles from the corner store. She taught all of us to be resourceful and creative. She also tried to give the three of us piano lessons. Larry always had a hard time sitting still, and he had a terrible sense of rhythm, yet he did learn how to play the drums when he was a little older. Kathy enjoyed music and wanted to experiment with other instruments. When she was in third grade, she took violin lessons, and later she joined the school orchestra.

My piano lessons didn't last much longer than Larry's had, as when I heard music I wanted to dance. I think I had been trying to dance ever since I was a toddler, so I begged for ballet lessons. I would have loved dancing lessons of almost any sort. While Kathy continued her violin lessons, Mother wouldn't let me have any dancing lessons. I used to be so angry about that. Other children were able to dance. Some of my friends at school were taking ballet lessons, and I envied them so much. As far as I was concerned, music and dance belong together, each one giving life to the other, and I so badly wanted to learn how to dance well. I dreamt of the Jackie Gleason Dancers and begged and begged Mother to let me have some lessons. Mother's reasoning, I later learned, was that she feared I would go off to Broadway of some such thing.

My mother loved to play the piano. She always had one with her whenever we moved. At home in the Orchard Avenue house, the piano she had played as a little girl was still in the foyer, where it had always been. She had a wide repertoire, including some of the famous classics, some songs from the musicals that were popular at that time, a little jazz, and some interpretations of popular songs, although she always said she didn't know that much.

She used to get lost in her music. The rhythms and melodies would carry her far from home for hours at a time. Then she would lose track of things going on in the household that may have needed her attention. There were some mishaps. However, Larry, Kathleen, and I always came through them just fine. No matter how engrossed she became with her music, Mother always had dinner ready at five o'clock every evening, when our dad came home from work. This was, at least in part, because she enjoyed cooking and experimenting with new recipes. She found recipe books almost as much fun to read as books that explained how to run your own business. She was always an avid reader and would often read two or three books at a time.

Our father always had mixed feelings about her piano playing. He liked some of the things she played, especially the jazz melodies he had worked on with his band. He had given up all his music when he came back home from his stint in the navy. Now he was an adult man with responsibilities. He would have appreciated it very much if his wife would simply give up the playthings of her youth and shoulder her responsibilities as his wife and the mother of their children. He would have been delighted if she had concentrated on mopping floors, hemming curtains, and ironing sheets.

My mother's parents had encouraged her to be independent from the time she was a little girl, so she could not imagine confining herself to trivial household chores. If the curtains at the windows fit well and were appropriate to the rooms they were in, she could see no reason to primp and fuss over them. Actually, she said that if the curtains matched, it was fine by her. I am certain that she put a little more attention into decorating than that, because she had a wonderful sense of color and proportion. She liked rich wood paneling on the walls and clean bold lines throughout her home. She believed that knickknacks only collected dust, so she would not permit them to be in her home. Our dad felt differently about this. He believed it was his wife's duty to stay at home, fuss over the house, and take care of him. Mother was a far more modern woman than that. She would happily do the necessary things at home, share her life with her husband and help him when he needed it, but she would not be his live in servant. She would have gone absolutely nutty with such a life.

Uncle Dan had picked out two acres on the side of the hill on his parents' Gibsonia property and begun to build there. My father, who worked with Dan and Bill every day at the sawmill, must have begun to see advantages himself in building on that property. Perhaps if his wife had a hand in designing their new home, she would be more contented to stay at home and keep it nice for him. Our parents decided not to hire an architect. Mother designed the layout of the house, drawing sketches and floor plans to illustrate what she wanted, and Dad, Uncle Dan, and Grandpap worked together to figure out how to build that house.

While Dad was proud of Mom's ability to do things, he should have realized that a woman who wanted to try her hand at building their home when she had never laid a brick or stone in her life would never be contented with household duties.

I was about three years old at the time, but I do remember my mother taking Larry, Kathy, and me out to the country during the day when Dad was at work. She laid many of those bricks for that basement by herself. Meanwhile, my sister, brother, and I ran wild through the woods. Larry used to love to climb trees. Six years old, he was small and light but fearless. To me, he appeared to be half monkey. He would happily have spent his life at the tops of the tallest trees. Kathy did her best to keep up with him, but I couldn't begin to do that. I would wander off, playing my own games, feeling as though I was out of their sight, when suddenly a nut would hit me on the back of my shoulder, or the top of my head. I would turn around and there Larry would be at the top of a tree, calling and shouting down to me. I was frustrated that I could not join him up there.

I had no idea what might be dangerous and what was not. Kathy and Larry had been climbing trees all afternoon, but I couldn't reach the branches as easily as my brother and sister could. That is, I couldn't reach them until I found this one tree with branches growing low to the ground. A pretty sort of vine with bright green leaves, tinged deep red at their tips and around the edges, was growing up the trunk of the tree. I played around that tree for quite a while and did manage to get up into its branches. Later that afternoon, I was covered with bright, red, itchy blotches. I scratched and wept, but the itches didn't go away.

My mother climbed up out of the basement foundation, took one look at me, and said, "Poison ivy." That evening when we were at home, she gave me a bath in cool water and put calamine lotion all over my spots, which were quite swollen by then. It almost made the itch go away, but I still felt miserable. Kathy and Larry laughed when they saw me covered nearly from head to toe with pink lotion, and I may have laughed with them. During the week the two of them brought their friends home to "look at Baby Beck!" Then everyone would laugh at me. I was always the compliant child, the child who did everything she was told to do. Kathy and Larry would call me out to show off my calamine lotion to all their friends. I twirled around and they laughed. I guess a three-year-old covered from head to toe with pink lotion does look pretty silly to a bunch of five- and six-year-olds.

Trouble or no, my mother was persistent. She took us back to the new house site almost every day, even though I did have poison ivy. She was intent on laying the brick for that basement and then building the chimney for the house. She had read a manual that described how to do this, and she and a good friend of hers by the name of Dot spent hours every day figuring out how to lay each brick so that we would have a working chimney.

Sometimes in the middle of the winter, when ice coated every branch and twig, the sun would come out and make the world glow and sparkle in every color imaginable. And when the leaves turned their bright oranges and reds in the fall, it was beautiful beyond words. Even so, living in the country must have been lonely for our mother, who loved being around people and thrived on the excitement of showing everyone how to make a large and complex project come together.

Mother and Dad worked together to build the rest of the house. We had three bedrooms on the same floor with the kitchen, living room, and dining room. The basement was quite large. In the 1960s, Mother had it finished it to make into more living space. It became a game room, or what some people call a den. Our house was starkly modern, especially when compared with any of the other houses in the neighborhood. The house had a flat roof and a large picture window in front, with clean, bold lines throughout.

Our parents had been married for about nine years when we moved out to Gibsonia. Even though the countryside can be beautiful out there, I am certain my mother felt isolated from many of the things that she loved. We were surrounded by woodland, and our neighbors all owned a few acres of land. Homes were tucked back behind the trees, and everything was so far away that few people attempted to walk anywhere. She could no longer walk to the grocery store to pick up our supplies, as it was nearly ten miles away. Even though most of the neighbors did not walk places, Mother still sent Kathy and Larry out to sell lemonade, telling them that cars still drove by and someone might stop to buy a cool drink. In time, she did get to know all the neighbors. The Hohmanns and the Schmiedals lived next door to us, and they had little girls who were my age. Mother started drawing again almost as soon as we settled in Gibsonia. I have a pastel of myself, and I couldn't have been more than three or four years old when she drew it. She drew pictures of Larry and Kathy as well. I believe the Hohmanns were the first of our neighbors who saw those portraits and liked them, so Mother offered to draw the Hohmann twins their portraits. Everyone liked her pictures. She even sold some to friends, who hung them in their homes. Then their friends saw them and ordered portraits of their children as well. This activity grew over the next couple of years, providing a tidy income for her. I was not in school when she started doing this, so I often went with her to people's homes. I liked doing this, because I always met new children to play with. She knew many stories and could make them up on the spot to suit the occasion. She discovered that if she could persuade the mother to leave her alone with the child for the next half hour or so, she could keep the little boy or girl contentedly entertained until she had drawn his likeness.

Mother charged about thirty dollars for each portrait that she drew, earning what might be called pin money from this activity. It was enough that we could take our laundry to the Laundromat every week.

Church became an important activity for her. Sunday mornings she would dress the three of us in our best. Often these were clothes she had made for us, little dresses with pretty lace trims on them for Kathy and me and pants and jacket sets for Larry.

Our brother was expansive and fun and he had a terrific sense of humor, but above all that he knew how to be loving and kind. A lot of very bright little boys are hyperactive. Their little bodies are meant to be out exploring the world and learning how it works, not cooped up in a classroom. At school, he was busily earning a reputation for being difficult to discipline. He would happily run and play, but sitting quietly to copy seemingly endless pages or adding and subtracting lists of numbers was tedious for him. His teachers found that getting him to do much of the work was nearly impossible, even though everyone who took the time to get to know my brother agreed that he was intelligent. If the classroom studies had included dancing on top of the desks, Larry would have won prizes.

At least, Larry behaved better when Mother was around, so she used to volunteer at the public school when we were in Bellevue and also in Gibsonia. Because of her artistic ability, the teachers were always glad to see her. She had a knack for putting classroom projects together in ways that were creative and fun for the children, and the teachers came to depend on her for the flare she had for making unique and eye-catching decorations. She volunteered at the Sunday school for the same reason. There she was a favorite with the teachers as she could and did make hymn singing exciting with her piano accompaniment. She could play "Rock of Ages" to a jazz beat that had everyone dancing.

My grandfather Gordon and uncle Dan loved our dad. They had been working together every day at the carpentry mill, and they believed he was a pretty good fellow. He was steady and hard working. They didn't see the tension building up at home between my parents. Anything my mother might have said about her problems would have sounded like complaining to them, so she kept quiet. In truth, Mother never was one to complain. Her father had taught both his children that he would not tolerate their squabbling or complaining. It was a lesson that she had learned well. The result for us was that while she liked to encourage us to talk with her reasonably and sensibly, she could not deal with any emotional displays from us—especially tears.

Our dad had a lot of nervous energy. He was a traditional German male in his thinking and sometimes known to be moody. To Mother, his storming about as he often did must have looked decidedly immature, causing her to want to treat him like a child. The feelings of affection and respect she had for him when they first married steadily deteriorated.

For several years, my mother tried to accommodate to her husband's demands, dutifully staying at home, attempting to take an interest in the kitchen curtains, and seeing how neat and spotless she could keep the living room floor. Mother would have dinner ready every day, as soon as our dad was home from work, and Larry, Kathy, and I would wash up and put clean clothes on, so that when our dad came in we would all be fresh and waiting for him. After dinner, our parents would sit out on the porch together. At first, they must have enjoyed each other's company, but as the years went by, they talked less and less. Our dad had little interest in the things that excited our mother. He was uncomfortable with her wanting to work outside the home. If her music and art projects drew her attention away from him, he wanted nothing to do with them. Mother simply wanted him to grow up and permit her to be an adult woman with interests and talents beyond housework. She needed challenges and creative outlets in order to feel properly alive.

Everyone who knew my dad thought he was a pretty good guy, and he was always patient and kind with me. And I clearly remember him happily giving what he could to people who had less than we did.

On Saturdays, Mother and Dad used to take us to visit friends. Usually we would just drive out and drop in, hoping the people we wanted to see were at home. Sometimes they took us out to Lake Erie Beach to go swimming or for a picnic.

Mother would cook and clean as quickly as possible in order to spend as much time as she could doing the things she loved. She always had an easel out with a painting in progress. I remember paintings of trees and rocks on a hill. That one must have impressed me, as I can easily visualize it after all these years. We had a large living room wall, about twenty feet long, which was perfect for murals. Mother painted quite a series of scenes on that wall. When we got tired of one picture, she painted another one over it. There was one jungle scene that we all liked, and it stayed up the longest.

Retreads or Hearing

THE SUMMER MOTHER TURNED TWENTY-SIX heralded a major turning point in all our lives. It was 1955. I was about four years old, Kathy was six, and Larry was seven. Mother and a friend of hers named Fran Cook had taken the three of us, along with Fran's two children, to the swimming pool. Mother loved to swim and was quite good at it. Larry, Kathy, and I were happily playing in a smaller pool, and no one had any idea that anything could be wrong. Fran and my mother must have been taking turns watching us while they swam. Until, in my mother's own words, "I swam down and became totally disoriented in the water. I became dizzy. I could not function. I could not move right. I couldn't get out of the pool. Fran, or the lifeguard, had to carry me out of the pool and physically carry me over to a wooden bench to lie down." This was an extremely frightening and confusing time for my mother, and it is not at all surprising that her memories of the event are hazy. It was the lifeguard who carried her out of the pool, as Fran would not have been able to do that by herself.

As far as my mother knew, this sudden attack could have been anything from polio to multiple sclerosis. Besides, swimming pools had been suspected as a vector for polio for a number of years. The lifeguard must have made a few emergency phone calls to make sure there would be enough lifeguards at the pool while he drove my mother home and carried her to bed. Fran drove all five of us children home, made sure Mother's car was returned to our house, and stayed with us to take care of Mother until our dad came home. Over the next couple of hours, Mother started to feel more like herself and found she was able to get up and move around, although she was still unsteady on her feet. When my father came home that evening, both he and Fran insisted that she see a doctor right away.

The first doctor she saw was a general practitioner. He believed that her unsteadiness and lack of coordination were due to an inner-ear infection. He gave her a prescription for eardrops, saying that they would clear it right up. Mother used the eardrops exactly as prescribed, and her dizziness came and went. Some days it was worse than others, but it didn't feel as though the problem was really going to go away with just the drops, so she decided to see a specialist. This doctor examined her ears and said that Mother appeared to have a condition of the inner ear that could not be cleared up with eardrops. However, if her condition was what he thought it was, it could be treated with surgery. He advised her to see another specialist, what she called a super-specialist, by the name of Dr. Lamp, who was one of the best ear surgeons in Pittsburgh. He gave her a thorough examination and said that she had what is known as otosclerosis. This meant that her inner-ear canal was hardening and becoming narrower with calcium and bone deposits. He did not offer my mother the happiest prognosis, saying that she would likely be totally deaf within a few years. However, there was a new surgical procedure, known as the Shea operation, designed to clean out the canal. Most people who had this did well with it, at least for a few years, until the boney deposits grew back.

For Mother, every day was stitched through and bound by the sounds of her children laughing, playing, and talking, as well as the music she loved. She could not imagine losing her hearing. Or rather, she *could* imagine it, and the thought was devastating. Her music meant a great deal to her, and giving that up would be like losing part of her soul.

She had been volunteering with the local public school, as Larry was hyperactive and difficult for the teachers to discipline. Even at home, he loved chaos. Pulling the tablecloth off the table in order to make the dishes fly all over the place was, to him, a big joke. He would laugh and jump up and down, gleefully looking about for anything else he could send flying, while the adults soberly cleaned up the mess. It is an art to take care of a little boy like that and teach him positive ways to use his energy. All his teachers agreed that he behaved better when Mother was there, so she volunteered at the Sunday school, where Larry went as well. Her volunteer work at both the school and church gave Mother great pleasure, and her heart broke when she realized that this work would have to end if she could not hear. Worst of all, she could not understand how she could take care of Larry, Kathy, and me at home if she could not hear us.

Dealing with the knowledge that her world would soon become silent was like facing death. Mother would not be permitted to have the surgery until she had lost a large percentage of her hearing, so those first two years after her diagnosis must have been the hardest of all for her. She forced herself to learn how to read lips, but that work left her feeling as though she had accomplished next to nothing, as even being able to read lips would not solve her problems.

Throughout that time, our dad was there, albeit mostly distant. Grandmother Gordon tried to be understanding, but thinking that the situation was either helpless or simply meant to be, she thought it best for her daughter to deal with this loss gracefully, and she had little patience for fussing. Our mother ought to learn how to bear her cross.

Oddly enough, Uncle Dan's wife Mabel was the only person Mother could confide in and who had the patience to commiserate with her. Aunt Mabel may have been very strict with her children, yet she also had a good heart where our mother was concerned and was emotionally there for Mother. She used to come over to our house every day, simply to be there while my mother went through what may have been for her the darkest time of her life. Once the diagnosis had been made, it seemed as though she began to lose her hearing rapidly. Mother was always telling us to speak more clearly, to look at her when we talked, and to please remember not to mumble or slur our words. Sometimes she had to tell us to speak in a lower register, as high tones were becoming hard for her to hear. These things can be difficult for a young child to master, but we could all see how frustrated she was, as she really wanted to know what we were saying.

However, Aunt Mabel was always there for her, offering a strong shoulder to cry on when she needed it. She patiently sat with her, silently mouthing passages out of books. My mother would watch, studying the infinitesimal changes Aunt Mabel's lips made as she mouthed the words in one of Mother's books. That was how Mother learned how to read lips. She put a tremendous effort into learning this, and eventually she could do it exceptionally well. I was not yet in school, so I was at home during the day. Sometimes I sat beside my mother, watching Aunt Mabel read, and I also learned how to read lips that year, though I could never do that as well as Mother could.

We were a lively bunch. I do recall one of our neighbors telling our mother that Larry was out in the bushes playing with a pack of matches. Fire can be fascinating for a young boy. A love of fire may be built in as part of our species. Mother had to do something that would get Larry's attention, immediately. She called the local fire department and told them to send a couple of their men over to give her son a good, firm talking-to. The fire marshal came over dressed in his uniform and badge. Mother said that Larry's little face turned white, that he was that frightened at the sight of this man. At least he never played with matches again. Larry had a friend who used to come over to the house to play and who thought it was great fun to pinch me to make me cry. I was only a baby at the time and not quite able to defend myself against a little boy who was bigger than I was. For all his wild ways, Larry was sweet, good-hearted, and protective of his sisters. Once he understood what was happening, he would not let that boy come near me.

During those years, Mother rethought everything about her life, assessing and analyzing the sorts of goals that would be possible for her with impaired hearing. She continued to paint during that time and play the piano. She also taught Kathy and I how to sew; she was a good seamstress as she made a lot of our clothes when we were toddlers.

Mother was an artist at heart. She loved to imagine how things could be and to see her ideas come to fruition. She had always had wonderful plans for our house in Gibsonia, putting up rich paneling on the walls and nicer frames around the windows and finishing the basement so that we could use it as living space. Dad earned a decent wage at the mill where he worked, but not quite enough to satisfy our mother's dreams for our home. Besides, Mother still had a most important vow to fulfill, the one that she had made as a very little girl, when she announced to her mother, at the age of five, that she would one day be a millionaire.

Some people might say that our mother was putting herself through too much stress, while others would say that she did the best thing she could do, when she got herself the job at Gimbels department store in the North Hills section of Pittsburgh. It was 1957, and it would be another year before she would be able to get the surgery on her ears. Hearing aids at that time were bulky, difficult to use, and did not differentiate sounds as well as they do now. People who hear well differentiate sounds without having to think about it each time they have to listen to people talking in a crowded room. Without having to think about it, they sort out the sounds of the people talking next to them and conversations from across the room. And of course every mother's head turns as soon as a baby cries or squeals, no matter how far away it is.

Larry, Kathy, and I were all in school at the time, so she felt this would be the best time for her to see what she could do out in a work setting with the hearing she still had. Besides, it would be an excellent way to hone her ability to read lips. At that time, Gimbels was one of the better quality department stores in Pittsburgh, so she was happy when they hired her to work in their paint department. Having to get up early, make sure her children got off to school safely, and then get herself to work on time for her first full-time job since her marriage ended her career of drawing portraits of the neighbors' children. To our mother it seemed like an important step to take in her effort to learn how to function with impaired hearing. She refused to allow this problem to prevent her from leading a full life.

At first, she caught a ride with one of her friends, who was going to and from work every day, but that couldn't go on indefinitely, and she had no intention of leaving that job. Fran Cook, the woman who had helped her the day her ears first started giving her trouble, had an old junker of a car that she said our mother could have for thirty dollars, the price she had been charging for her portraits. It was a 1941 Ford. Perhaps you've heard the old acronym that F-O-R-D stands for Fix or Repair Daily. This had to have been the car that gave birth to that saying. The car should have been taken to the auto graveyard ages before Fran sold it to our mother. It leaked oil, badly. Black smoke would billow from the exhaust everywhere she drove, and Mother had to keep cans of oil handy in the backseat, as every few miles she had to stop to add another quart to the crank case so the engine wouldn't freeze. My mother recalled having to do this every time the car made a bad noise. There was a window in back that rattled in its track and fell out, if it wasn't held in place. Larry, who was about ten years old at the time, had the honor of sitting beside that window to make sure it didn't fall out. This was a very important job on cold winter days. He was proud of being able to help our mother this way. His other job was to climb up into the front seat and hold his foot on the gas pedal, while Mother went up under the hood to pour some gas into the uptake line to prime the carburetor. When Larry was at school, Mother wedged a baseball bat over the gas pedal so that she could prime the engine without our help.

Kathy was supremely embarrassed to be seen riding in this car. Her friends used to make fun of it, or at least she thought they did. If she had to ride in that car, she would crouch down as close to the floor of the backseat as she could get, huddled in a corner out of the way of all those cans of oil, so that no one would be able to see her through the windows. I was still pretty little at the time. All I knew was that I was riding with my mother, my big sister, and my brother and that was the way things were.

Most women would have likely given up on that car as well as the job, especially if their husbands were putting pressure on them to stay at home. But not our mother. She used that car for quite a while to get to and from work, the grocery store, or wherever else she had errands to run. She even used it to pull stumps out of their lot on the Gibsonia property. That car was sixteen years old at that time and trying to die. Mother very determinedly nursed it along for three or four more years.

She worked at Gimbels for about a year, until she came down with a bad case of the flu and had to stop. However, this job had given her a few precious things. First, it gave her the opportunity to test her strength and ability against great odds. Just getting to and from work was a terrific test. Second, it had her out working with other people. She began to learn how to be a saleswoman during that time, and she also learned the difference between having a job to earn money and building a career. And she did this at a time when her hearing was noticeably deteriorating.

Learning to live with only partial hearing can be a trial. Even a person who hears well cannot understand what someone else is saying entirely, especially when he is overtired or not paying good attention. This is because, even in the best of situations, we tend to hear only parts of the words spoken to us. It is only because we know what the words are supposed to sound like that we are able to make sense of them and understand what the other person is saying. Someone who has partial hearing is able to hear less of what is being said, and if he is not paying strict attention, he might think the other person said something entirely different from what he meant, or even something nonsensical. It is also true that hearing loss is selective. High-pitched voices and tones are the first to go. There are plenty of jokes about wives who believe their husbands don't want to hear what they have to say, when in truth their husbands cannot hear them. There are even nursery rhymes making fun of hearing loss. A very old one goes:

Old woman, old woman, shall we go a shearing?
Speak a little louder, sir. I'm very thick o' hearing.
Old woman, old woman, shall I kiss you dearly?
Thank you, kind sir. I hear very clearly.

The people she worked with had a tendency to either make fun of her inability to hear or to insist that she had not been paying attention. They may not have been malicious, but it was a very real problem at Gimbels, as she had to face the public every day as well as forge relationships with her coworkers and her boss.

Perhaps if our dad had been able to empathize with her, she would have been able to withstand the jokes and barbs directed toward her from people who were relative strangers. A woman expects that the man she marries will be her closest friend and ally. He is the one person she should be able to trust above all others. When this does not work out, when the man she marries proves that he cannot be trusted this way, she feels betrayed. Our dad seldom expressed anything but impatience over Mother's inability to hear and her need for surgeries. Thus, she was deeply hurt over the unkind things people said, such as, "Oh, she only hears what she wants to hear" or "She needs to pay better attention."

In 1958, the doctor told her that she had lost enough hearing that she would be a good candidate to have what was then known as a stapedectomy, or the Shea procedure, named after the surgeon who had developed the technique to clean out excess bone growth in ear canals. For years, Dad had been telling our mother that she should stay at home and take care of the house and children. He didn't want her to be off trying to earn money with her drawing or playing the piano in restaurants, as she had started to talk about doing, if her surgery turned out successful. Perhaps losing her hearing, harsh as that may be, was God's way of telling her that she needed to be a proper wife and mother. He claimed that the money would be better spent on new tires for the car. After all, he did need a dependable vehicle to get to and from work every day.

Mother was devastated over this. Tension had been building up between my parents over the last few years. There had been a series of low-level arguments that never reached breaking point but that were never resolved or healed. For Mother, Dad's attitude about her hearing loss was the last straw. Mother was even more brokenhearted when even Grandmother Gordon said she agreed with Dad. "Well, he does need to be able to get to and from work."

"He can get retreads. I need to be able to hear!"

The world had not changed to the extent Grandma Gordon had hoped, years ago when she stood up to her father and brother in order to go to nursing school. Women still had to listen to their husbands, and whether he was right or wrong, Verne was Helen's husband. As his wife, it was her duty to do what he said. Grandma had always been one to acquiesce to her family's needs, and Mother, from the time she was a little girl, had been more strong minded than a lot of children. Grandma may have wondered whether she should have disciplined her daughter more when she was a child. Instead, she had always encouraged her daughter's independence and strength of will. When Helen was a little girl, her mother would do her best to give her everything she could. Once, as a treat for a special occasion, she ironed one of Helen's blouses with rows of pin-pleats going down the front and sleeves. Mother thought they were so nice that she insisted all her blouses should be ironed that way.

Now, as far as Grandma Gordon was concerned, her daughter was demanding to have something that might be neither safe nor possible. From a medical standpoint, this was an experimental operation. Anything could go wrong. Goodness knew she would have given all she had to help her daughter hear again, but she had seen what was inside the ear canal. Microscopic bones must somehow be preserved in order for the operation to offer any hope of success, and the operative site's proximity to the brain was too frightening to contemplate. One slip of a scalpel and her daughter could lose far more than her hearing. Due to her fear of a new and dangerous operation, she believed our dad should use the money to put tires on his car.

Meanwhile, our mother was struggling to maintain who and what she was. Many women have stayed home and just taken care of their homes and families, believing that this was what they were meant to do. Some women thrive in that role. Then there are other women, whom we have all seen, who become excessively controlling. Everything must be just so and everyone around them must be prepared to jump to her bidding whenever she raises her little finger.

People have often said of such women that they should be CEOs in charge of corporations, that they have more energy and more organizational skills than the job of housewife and mother would require. Then there are women who quietly go nutty when they are isolated from other adults and prevented from participating in the community. We call this cabin fever. Mother wanted no part of any of that. As far as she was concerned, this was when her marriage with our dad ended. I will always believe that my dad felt differently about their marriage. I know that he was brokenhearted as she gradually retreated from their relationship. He did try, in his clumsy way, to repair the damage of not recognizing her hearing problem, but for Mother the damage was done.

Dr. Lamp operated first on one ear, and a few weeks later she went back to the hospital to have the other ear canal cleaned out. The results were good, and she was able to hear, at least for a couple of years. Then she had to go back to have her inner-ear canals cleaned out again. She ultimately went in so many times for those operations that she lost count of them. Dad went with our mother the first time she was hospitalized for that procedure, but he never expressed any interest in how she faired. After that, he didn't go with her at all. My parents did not have any health insurance then, so they had to pay cash for all those surgeries.

In that same year, 1958, a new pastor, Rev. Richard Morledge, began to lead services at the Bakerstown Presbyterian Church, where our family had been going since we moved to Gibsonia. He traveled from house to house within the community, introducing himself to all his parishioners, and was very happy to discover that our mother was an artist. Everyone who saw her paintings was impressed. He asked if Mother would be willing to decorate the altar for Christmas. If what he had in mind was drama and elegance, he could not have gone to a better person. The first project she did for him was a poinsettia wreath. A twenty-foot cross stood behind the pulpit at that time. Mother designed the wreath to go all around that cross. She carefully mounted sections of pegboard so that they would completely frame the cross, and to that frame she attached pine limbs and pinecones.

Every four feet, all around the wreath, she fixed a poinsettia plant. She did not simply arrange the flowers, she attached the pot to the framework, carefully arranging layers of pine boughs around it, so all anyone would be able to see would be the flame-colored flowers highlighting the greenery. Reverend Morledge was not at all certain the entire wreath would not come tumbling down on top of him in the midst of his sermon. Visions of death by wreath must have assailed him, for he asked our mother numerous times whether this project would succeed. To his surprise and relief, the wreath did not collapse during his services. It was a spectacular view behind him as he spoke his sermon.

Mother's next project for the church was for Easter. It was a scene of Jesus and his disciples painted on pressboard, so large that it had to be carried to the church in sections and put together there. Once the boards had been mounted together, they depicted a larger-than-life-size vision of Christ and the apostles in bold colors. Everyone said it was beautiful, and the church was able to use it for many years. During this time, she continued to volunteer. What made her even happier was that she was able to go back to volunteering at Larry's classes at the Sunday school and the public school. Mother's love of volunteering led her to become a Girl Scout leader when I was in elementary school.

Music for my mother was a way to heal and enrich her soul. She loved to play, and now that she could hear again she played every day, becoming quite skillful and building a nice repertoire of pieces, although she always claimed she didn't really know that much about music. For all she had been a little wild as a teenager, she had still led a sheltered life. She had no idea what a supper club was, or a so-called after-hours club, or the differences between those two sorts of establishments and a saloon. She thought it would be fun to play piano at the sort of restaurant that hired people to entertain this way. It was 1960. By then, Mother had received another couple of operations on each of her ears and eagerly wrapped herself in her music, an old friend that she valued even more after being forced to leave it for a while. Having her music taken away through one of nature's mistakes and then having it returned through surgery was little short of a miracle. Otosclerosis is a progressive condition. While the Shea operation proved to be a blessing for those people who could receive that surgery, the procedure needed to be performed every few years, depending on how quickly bone matter grew back to fill the inner-ear canal and block all sound. Inevitably the surgery would no longer help those people. This knowledge weighed at the back of our mother's mind, making her feel almost frantic. She would work as much and live as much as she possibly could, for tomorrow she might be profoundly deaf.

I am certain this experience also increased her sense of urgency as far as earning money was concerned, for without money she would not be able to get the sort of help she might need should the worst happen and she would no longer be able to hear anything again.

In order to earn money as a piano player, one had to belong to the musicians union. My mother went to Pittsburgh, about twenty-five miles from where we lived, to register with that union. I believe she thought of this a little as a joke, as though she couldn't really call herself a musician. Making music was something she loved to do, but she never considered her playing much more than entertainment for her friends and family. Even so, people appreciated what she played, and she always enjoyed being the center of attention. "When I play the piano, people stop talking and they listen to me."

The first job she found was at an after-hours club in Pittsburgh known as The Harp and Crown. My mother had never heard of such a place until she began to look around for work as a piano player. She played mostly on weekends, from eleven o'clock at night until two or even three in the morning. Dad occasionally went with her to keep her company, but for the most part she worked alone. She would go in, sit down, and play, and all that she was aware of was that people were eating and drinking and enjoying her music. Still, she had never expected to work such late night hours. Years later, she said of that time, "I don't know how I did it."

At home, when Mother practiced, she would forget that the real world was still out there. I was nine years old, and Kathy and Larry were eleven and twelve. We were at the age when we were beginning to become involved in after-school activities. Such things as scout meetings for me, violin lessons for Kathy, and athletics for Larry kept us busy and guaranteed that one or another of us would need to be chauffeured here or there a few times each week. Mother would drop us off at our meetings and then go back home and sit down in front of her piano to play her heart out. The minutes would become hours and she would continue to play the piano. Perhaps the sun going down compelled her to turn the light on so she could see the notes. It was not until she had looked up at the clock that she would remember, *Kathy is standing out in the snow in front of the school, waiting for me.* Then she would go to the car and navigate her way to the school to pick up Kathy from her weekly violin lessons. Often this did not happen, and Kathy would walk home after her lessons because there was no way to call Mother on the phone to remind her that Kathy was waiting for her. I wasn't taking music lessons at school, but occasionally Mother forgot that she had left me at a church function, and I would be standing outside, waiting for what felt like hours, until she remembered that I was not in the house and that I could not get myself home.

Sometimes it wasn't too bad, as the school was close enough that we could walk back to the house, if we had to. However, at best it would be a couple of hours before we were home again, and we didn't want to miss Mother if she did happen to come while we were hiking down the road. Other times, we were lucky that a friend would pick us up and bring us home. All Mother would say at those times was, "So sorry." We all understood this was the way she was and there was no point in getting angry over it.

All that practicing did build up her skill as a piano player. When she worked at the supper club, she played continuously for forty minutes, taking a break long enough to use the restroom or get a bite to eat and then go back to play again for another forty minutes.

She liked to think of the supper club where she worked as being a high-end restaurant. However, Grandmother Gordon was scandalized that her daughter would stoop to play in such a place. Grandpap

Gordon had been a heavy drinker for years, creating problems for everyone who cared about him. As far as Grandma Gordon was concerned, it was and always had been up to the wife and mother to set the moral tone within the household. If her man drank—especially if her man drank—it was the woman's job to keep herself pure of such vices and not work in an establishment that encouraged drinking.

I am not certain whether Aunt Mabel contributed her voice to this, or what she may have said if she did, but I do know that Mother's piano-playing career at the supper club did not last very long, a year at most. She enjoyed attending functions that the musicians union put on for its members. I remember going to a couple of them with her. Larry, Kathy, and I would join her at the annual musicians union Christmas parties.

Breaking the Glass Ceiling

DURING THE SECOND WORLD WAR, when Mother was in high school, women were expected to work outside the home. Most of the able-bodied men were fighting overseas, and women considered it their duty to contribute all the skills they had in order to support the war effort. Helen's mother had worked as a nurse during those years and had always been proud to be able to do so. Even though Grandpap Gordon would have preferred his wife be at home taking care of household matters, he had always understood that the work she did was necessary. He was proud of her for being a good nurse.

When the war ended and the men came home, women were advised to return to their kitchens so that there would be jobs for the men returning to civilian life after the fighting. Mother had grown up seeing her mother work, and she assumed that she should be taken seriously in the workaday world, just as her mother had. In the early 1960s, women had not yet begun to re-enter the work force in great numbers. Of course there were teachers and nurses, but the glass ceiling, as it later came to be known, had settled firmly in place and was difficult to break through. Women whose ambitions lay beyond taking orders from the men in their lives generally had to struggle. The women who thrived in the workplace soon learned that if they were going to succeed at what they did, they would have to prove they could do the job at least as well as, if not better than, their male colleagues. Women could not afford to be too modest about telling their bosses what they could accomplish. This was something our mother seemed to understand almost instinctively.

Mother got a job at a weekly advertising paper in Milvale called

Greensheet. The owner, Milt Hammond, hired her as a layout artist. People liked her work, but Milt didn't pay her much for it, and although she was able to do a lot of it at home it did not satisfy her desire for a real income. She and Dad were not getting along well, and I believe she was beginning to wonder how she would support us if the two of them did separate. Whether she wanted to consider it that way or not, money would be necessary to keep her children comfortable. After she had been there for a few months, she went to Milt to ask for a job in sales.

"What, our little artist wants to be a salesman? What do you know about sales?"

Many women would have been cowed down right then, needing time to rebuild their confidence or choosing not to approach their boss again. However, Mother was never that sort of person.

"Well, you might be losing a lot of money if you don't hire me. You might be losing a million dollars or so."

Milt liked her show of confidence. He figured that the worst that could happen was that she would fall flat on her face. With that sort of can-do attitude, it could be worth his while to give her a try. She told me years later that she had first offered to work for him for free, but that he insisted he could not hire her for nothing, so he gave her a small wage until she could prove herself.

My mother went downtown and bought herself a suit and two dresses so that she would look respectable, and then she set to work. At the end of the first week, Milt asked her, in front of all the other employees, how she was doing. She pulled a sheaf of papers out of her briefcase and read off all the places she had called and the sales she had made. The guys stood there cheering her on, and Milt began to get embarrassed. "Now, that's enough," he said.

"I'm not finished yet."

So he listened, and he must have been impressed, for he acted as though he was rather surprised that she had sold so many ads and kept her records in such a businesslike way.

Going out to meet all those business owners was exciting for her. With each interview, she thought about what worked well and what had not and used what she had learned with her next interview. The forthright confidence that she had shown Milt Hammond that first day served her well every time she went out to meet a new client.

Many very intelligent people have a difficult time keeping track of the people they just met. Mother was phenomenal in this way. She remembered clearly even those people she had met for only a few moments, weeks or even months before. Besides this, she was such a gracious and witty conversationalist that people remembered her.

People often said that our mother's ambition and determination to succeed were unusual in a woman. Perhaps those traits were unusual in women of her generation, but it would be wrong to say that those are not qualities that women can and have developed in many different ways, throughout history.

Balancing family life and work life is a never-ending puzzle for working moms and dads all over the world. Our dad had always made it a point to be at home by five thirty every evening, no matter what might be going on at the mill. The rush orders could wait, he thought. Being with his family was more important. Our mother was paid by the sales she made, and that put pressure on her to make as many of those sales as she could. Besides, she was attempting to build a career. She would not come home early if the only time she could meet with a client was in the evening after his workday was done. She understood better than many women do that in order to impress her colleagues she would have to do better work than they did. I remember overhearing phone conversations—Mom would call up to say she would be late for dinner and Dad would shout at her, "Why can't you be at home with your family?"

I am certain it was embarrassing for her to have to deal with this in front of a client. This was well before the days when you could call home on your cell phone, from the privacy of your car as you barrel down the highway, on your way from one appointment to another. She must have been making these calls from pay phones, or perhaps from a phone in her client's office. Still, embarrassment or not, she usually made her sale.

It can be very difficult to develop a salable skill and then prove to the rest of the world that you have that skill so that you can earn a living by it. Had our parents' marriage been a happy one, Mother might have chosen to develop her art, taking her portraits to galleries and building shows around her work, or she might have chosen to develop her music so that she could play in small orchestras and ensembles. That was not to be. Dad had a low tolerance for the things our mother loved to do, when those things interfered with the care of their home.

For all her love of art and her wonderful creative ability, Mother was pragmatic. Jobs for artists, at least jobs that were likely to pay a living wage to a woman, were rare. It can take years of persistence to build up a real career as an artist. The idea we have of the starving writer or painter eking out a living in his freezing garret is based on fact. From the time she was little, Mother had determined to earn enough money to be comfortable and independent. Sales appeared to be a much more direct road toward that goal than promoting her painting and music.

During the last few months of their marriage, our mother and father gradually stopped talking to each other. This must have been painful for both of them. Mother always appreciated good conversation, and our dad really did want their marriage to work. As with most children, I liked it best when my parents were together. Kathy and Larry felt differently about it, as our dad had been critical of them. When she was a teenager, Kathy did look a lot like our mother had when she and Dad first met. I may have reminded Dad of his family, or perhaps the problems he had with Kathy and Larry made a deeper impression on me than I thought. I now know that he was deeply hurt that he and his wife did not get along. I know now, from seeing my friends go through marital upsets, that neither party is completely villainous. We all make mistakes and we all have been guilty of saying and doing things that in an ideal world would never be said or done.

My father had a wonderful sense of humor that all his friends appreciated, and he did want to show us that he cared. On weekends, he took us to visit his parents, who were still living in the same townhouse on Tripole Street in Northside, Pittsburgh, when our parents were first married. Grandpa Gebauer had suffered a stroke a few years before, so by the time we were able to get to know him, he was spending most of his day on the living room couch, where Grandma Gebauer took care of him. She did introduce us to German foods that she had liked when she was little. All Grandma Gebauer knew how to cook was German food.

In our mother's words, she and Dad struggled together for a few more years, becoming cross, sullen, and silent toward each other as time went on. This continued until 1962. Kathy and Larry were both in the ninth grade and I was in seventh grade. According to Mother's recollection, we had been sitting down to supper together when Larry, waving his arms around in his excitement to say something, spilt a glass of water on the table. Mom said that Dad became excessively upset over this. I don't remember any of that. She described Larry in this way. "He wasn't being bad. He just he was so exuberant. Whenever he would talk, he would wave his arms around. And as he got older, he would wave his bigger arms around." She, of course, tried to defend her son from any temper outbursts, and our dad finally said, "Well, that's it. I'm out of here."

Talking about this, Kathy and I remembered another version of the separation. Larry and our mother were sitting at the piano playing a duet together. Dad walked in and lost his temper over something, it could have been anything. Kathy and Larry were both relieved when he walked out, promising not to come back. I was devastated.

Whatever the argument was that finally tipped the scales, this is the dialogue which occurred that day, according to Mother. She must have felt a sense of relief when he announced he was leaving, for she coolly replied, "That's good. Do what you want."

Dad had put his foot in it, but he wasn't going to back down. "I'm never coming back."

"Well, that's fine. Go to your mother. If I need you, I'll call you."

"That's it."

"What's done is done."

Until he remarried, Dad made a point of seeing us regularly and taking us places whenever he could. He seemed to have friends everywhere he went.

I remember Kathy, Larry, and I having issues as we watched our mother put money into her own wardrobe—dresses, shoes, and handbags—so she could impress her clients, while her children went without some of the things that we needed for school, such as new tennis shoes. Reflecting back, she had two or three dresses and one pair of heels in her closet. Perhaps I think we were just not accustomed to Mother buying clothes for herself. Maybe we wanted to think of our mother as an artist. After all, that is what many of the arguments had been about when she and our dad were living together. Now she was putting her heart and soul into selling stuff, ads for a newspaper.

To help the family and bring more income, Larry got a job with a lawyer who owned a farm next to Treesdale Orchard, where he worked during summers and on holidays. Our neighbor, Buzz Quiren, who helped Larry get the job, took him to work at five am and returned at five pm. He baled hay, took care of the rabbits, and milked the cows. The work was hard and dirty, but Larry was energetic and eager to please. On his own initiative, he often did repairs and other jobs he saw that needed doing. At the end of each week, Larry would hand over his paycheck to our mother. We often saved our school lunch money, forty cents a day, to spend on other things. When Mother saw us with that little bit of cash, she would borrow it back in order to buy gas and a few groceries.

Larry's grades began to drop during the tenth grade, and he stopped listening to our mother. So many teenage boys have similar problems; it is almost a rite of passage. The lawyer Larry had been working for proved to be an excellent friend. He thought of our brother as being highly intelligent, generous, and hard working. He could see that there were some problems and he wanted to help mend them. Perhaps, he thought, the discipline of a good military school would get Larry onto a good track. They decided on Greenbrier Military School, down in West Virginia, which had an excellent record, and he offered to pay half the tuition if Mother could pay the other half. She talked with our dad about helping out with this expense, but he had recently remarried, and his new wife was not happy that he wanted to help to support his first family. He was sorry, but he could not help Larry that way. Mother took out loans to cover that expense. She used the house we were living in as collateral on those loans.

At times we didn't have enough food for our supper, because Mother had not had time to take one of us to the store. Kathy and I had to fill in a lot, doing the cooking and housework that Mother no longer had time to do every day, in addition to our schoolwork. When I look back on those times, I don't remember the hardship. What I do remember, though, is the love and support we received from our grandmother. She was always so sweet about making sure we had what we needed that I looked forward to those days when we had to go to her house lunch or supper. Those years taught me that above all, family is most important; building those ties and keeping them strong is holy work.

Sales work offered Mother the chance to earn more money, but in order to be in the business world she needed one or two decent dresses. Without a wardrobe that projected a successful businesswoman, people would too easily assume that what she was selling was not a quality product or that she was not conducting herself in a businesslike manner. She did buy a couple of *Vogue* patterns and some good wool fabric, and from those she made herself some very nice suits.

Mother began taking over the work at Milt Hammond's office. She would organize the projects and make sure things were done on time. She may not have been perfect at what she did when she started, but it provided an excellent learning experience. Whether it was because Mother was a woman or because she did not have a degree in business management, Milt never did pay her much for what she did. Many employers of that era stated categorically that women did not have families to support, as men did, and therefore did not need the money. Mother continued to take on responsibility at Milt

Hammonds. Knowing my mother, it is difficult to imagine her not running whatever she was involved with and doing so competently. He apparently approved of her running his office, but he didn't want to pay her much for the duties she had taken on.

In 1965, Milt Hammond introduced our mother to Ron Northey. He was a good looking man, square jawed and forceful, who knew how to be suave and sophisticated. Besides this, he had been well known as a Major League Baseball player for many years, with the Cincinnati Red Sox and the Pittsburgh Pirates. Mother used to say of him, "He was a ballplayer that everyone knew, and of course I wasn't interested in baseball, so I started seeing him." She had gone out on dates with a few different men, but no one really excited her. Ron Northey was demanding and inordinately interested in himself. But he could also be very nice and a lot of fun, and he was good to our mother. I suspect she found him interesting because of his service in the army during WWII. He was also somewhat deaf in one ear, and therefore he could likely empathize with our mother's hearing problem. I was excited by the fact that he was so well known, although by the late 1950s he had essentially retired from active playing. He had coached the Pittsburgh Pirates until 1963. Everyone who liked baseball knew about Ron Northey and thought it was exciting that Mother was dating such a well-known man. People tended to stay married longer than they do now, no matter how ugly things might have been behind closed doors. They looked down on those who were divorced more than they do now. They believed that when one married, one made a promise to stay with the other person no matter what might happen. Only people with awful character defects would ever divorce. Thank goodness that is not the way we see things now. Both divorcees, Mother and Ron understood this, and Ron seemed like a nice fellow. At the same time, I was unsure I wanted him in the house. At one time he came to dinner, and I said to him, "Where are you going to sit? We don't have a chair for you." Mother was upset with me for that comment.

Ron also had some negative things to say about Larry going to military school, and the way Mother was raising us in general.

He claimed she had not taught us to be respectful toward adults. According to him, we were supposed to address her as *ma'am* or *Mother* and to call men *sir*. Those things didn't bother me, but I don't know what Kathy and Larry thought of them. Ron wanted Mother to give all her attention to him. I knew what I would have said to any of my friends had they been so domineering, and we knew what our mother would have said to any of us had we demanded all her energy, as Ron was doing. She put up with it from him, as did the rest of us. She really did like him. In some ways, he must have reminded her of her father, as both of them were domineering men who could be very kind to the people they cared about. Besides, from the time she was quite little she had been able to deal with her father.

She got a kick out of going to the country club with Ron, where she met his select crowd of friends. Years later, she told me that she only had one dress that was fit to wear on a date with him, and she wore it repeatedly. She thought he must be bored with it. He and his friends used to play bridge a lot. My mother had never played the game before, yet she surprised him by learning to play it within a few sessions. It never seemed like a difficult game to her, and she considered it dull. Ron loved to play bridge, and he was either inviting his friends over to play or heading to their homes for a game. Sometimes Mother would play hostess and prepare a buffet in his home for all his bridge-playing friends. She always had liked to cook, and these games gave her a chance to show off her skill and experiment with fancier recipes than she usually made for us at home. She would make soufflés and fine sauces for Ron and his friends.

Larry was at military school, and things did seem a bit lonesome for Kathy and me. We all missed Larry. He was a smart, generous, energetic, and fun-loving young man who saw how ridiculous so many things in our lives were and could easily make us laugh about everything, including our troubles.

When he wasn't playing cards or baseball, Ron was playing golf, nearly every weekend, except in the dead of winter. My mother began to play golf with him and enjoyed getting out in the sun and fresh air. Even though he didn't get along wonderfully with her children, to her he was a very attractive man. That is, until his former wife came back into the picture. Whatever it was that caused their divorce, whether it was his jealousy or his inability to understand their children, his wife decided to put it all behind her and wanted him back. That was the last our mother saw of Ron Northey and his friends. Mother was devastated. It is always difficult to go back to being single once a man has been seriously courting you. She had to go back to the everyday world of knowing there would not be a man to fuss over and support her through difficult times, knowing that the whole of her life was squarely back on her shoulders. We wanted to cheer our mother up when her birthday came around that year. Besides, we all had dreams of her marrying someone who had a little money. The three of us had visions of owning a swimming pool and perhaps a boat—at least those are the sorts of things Mother heard us talking about. We put all our resources together that year, any coins we could scrounge from doing extra chores, saving our lunch money instead of eating at school, and managed to get our mother a new bathing suit for her birthday. It was cut very low in back, one of the newest styles for the late 1960s and rather daring by Mother's standards. It certainly was not the sort of gift she would have expected from us, but she did wear it. We hoped that with any sort of luck, that bathing suit would attract the attention of some nice man who owned a boat and a swimming pool and who would want to put our mother in them once he saw how fetching she looked.

Kathy and Mike Stermon were high school sweethearts who married after school. Mike joined the navy and would soon be serving on the USS *Hornet,* an airline carrier, the same ship our uncle had served on when he was in the navy. The two of them were very much in love. That is how our mother met Vernie Stermon, Mike's mother. After the break from Ron, Mother had more time to be at home and Vernie and Mother became good friends. Mother was never one to sit around letting depression, especially depression over a man, take over her life. Within a few weeks, she was playing golf with Vernie Stermon, and they had some delightful times together. The two of them would mix up martinis in their thermoses to drink while they were playing so as not to get dehydrated.

Mother found a job working for an ad agency called Goldman, Schoop, and Rothschild. She was proud of the way she went about getting that job. The agency was run by a group of Jewish businessmen, so she went to all the clients she'd had before, who were Jewish, and asked for references. She worked for this agency for a year or so, directing television commercials and playing the part of a piano player in some of those commercials. Her work life there was rich and interesting and a wonderful learning experience. She was working hard and was enjoying herself. Still, this job offered more by way of prestige than money. The next job she had, with Reuben Donnelly Yellow Pages, was also a remarkable learning experience, as advertising was what they did. They were the company that had originally started the Yellow Pages, now part of every phone book. Here again, the main focus was on selling ad space.

Mother's dream had always been to run a business of her own. When I was growing up, she must have read a few hundred books about how to establish and manage a successful business. It seemed to me that she read everything that was in print in those days. I do recall seeing Dale Carnegie's *How to Win Friends and Influence People* by her place at the table. She had books about business piled on the nightstand by her bed, and she had more books on the end table by the couch in the living room. When I leafed through any of them, I would find that she had marked and underlined passages. She never had any doubt in her mind that she would have to work for what she wanted. On the other hand, she always believed that she could succeed, as long as she had access to the information she needed and even half a chance to try out her ideas.

For a while, she had thought about running a car wash. I remember Mother taking us to a car wash, sitting in the car with her and Kathy and Larry, counting all the cars that went through the wash. One of us was supposed to count the cars that went through twice, another was supposed to keep track of the cars that used the vacuum equipment to clean out the insides, and one of us was supposed to count the cars that received an extra polish at the end. However, for whatever reasons, she decided that opening a car wash might not be the best thing to do.

Throughout her life, Mother had never had a lot of money. Her parents had been frugal about everything. The mill where her father, brother, and husband worked had supported them fairly well but by no means luxuriously. After her divorce, Mother had to make every penny count just to keep food on the table and to make sure we had what we needed for school. During the years Kathy, Larry, and I were in high school, it was very tight. My sister and I were about the same size, so we shared many of our clothes. It was tight, but we managed to get through those years, and I have countless wonderful memories from that time. Those were the years when I really learned to care about my family.

We were growing up and beginning to move on. Working at a job was what Mother did, because she had to in order to earn money. It was important to her to be able to make things comfortable for all of us. However, at this time, Kathy had a baby and was busily forging on with her new family in Tennessee. Larry was at Point Park College in downtown Pittsburgh, which was close by, so he frequently came back to see us. I was in my last year of high school and I had already enrolled at Park Point College for the fall semester. Mother's office was located in East Liberty, and she had never enjoyed the commute back and forth to Gibsonia, as beautiful as the countryside could be. She thought she would sell the house there and move to an apartment near where she worked.

Mother was doing well with Rueben Donnelly Yellow Page Sales, and although she wasn't earning the sort of money she would have liked, her expenses started to go down as we started to build our own lives. It looked as though things could get a little easier for Mother. She bought a brand-new Pontiac LeMans. It was the first new car she had ever owned, and she loved the sense of luxury and class it gave her.

Then the floor fell out from under her. This was the middle of winter. The roads were covered with patches of ice, and even when you are not stressed and you are paying excellent attention to the road and what is in front of you, accidents do happen. She skidded into a guardrail on her way to an interview with one of her clients. She had not owned the car for more than a few months, and now it was gone. She wasn't hurt, at least not badly, but what really shook her up was the fact that she still had to pay for the car, as her accident insurance had run out.

Uncle Dan, who had always been close with our mother, gave her a car he no longer needed, an old Rambler. He told her she could use it until she got back on her feet. The car was a godsend, as it enabled Mother to continue working, but it truly was a comedown for her. She probably would not have minded so much driving her brother's car if she had not been sending a check every month to pay for the car of her dreams, which was no more.

Most of the women I know would have been devastated by that turn of events. When she described that situation to me, her final comment was "Well, what's done is done." She had simply picked up and gone on with her life. "Simply" might not be the best word here. It takes inner strength to keep on going when unpleasant things happen. Most of us instinctively pull back, wanting a break from our responsibilities, even if only for a short while, in order to let ourselves heal emotionally. Often circumstances, as well as our concepts of how our lives should be running, will not permit that.

Mother could not conceive of stopping to rest, not then. However, she did make it a point to make a few new friends and have some fun. At least once or twice a week she would go out to a singles dance that a few of the hotels in Pittsburgh took turns sponsoring. As far as the money went, the only way Mother could see to get through this trouble was to sell the house she and our dad had built in Gibsonia. With the proceeds from the sale she could pay the taxes, finish paying the loans she had taken out so that Larry could go to the Greenbrier Military School in West Virginia, pay what she still owed on the car, and put in a down payment on a condominium in East Liberty.

She did not want to pay a real estate agent's fee, as this would prevent her from earning enough to pay the back taxes on the house and the debt on her car. So she researched the legal paper filing that would be necessary and interviewed people who knew the legal ins and outs of selling a house, so she could do it herself. She successfully sold the house and paid those debts.

Kathy was now living with her new family in California, and Larry would be leaving in October to join the navy. Mother, Larry, and I moved in with Grandma so that Mother could clear everything out of the house. Mother and I slept in what had been Aunt Mary's bedroom, and Larry camped on the couch in the living room. That little cabin felt really crowded. Nevertheless, Grandma made us feel welcome there, just as she always had.

Road Trip

SHORTLY BEFORE SHE MET ROBERT De Young, her second husband, Mother had a dream that she would meet someone who would be very special to her and whose name would have the initials D. Y. She did meet a fellow by the name of David Young at one of the dances she had been going to. That fellow was looking for a mother for his children, and he proved to be almost anything but interesting. Our mother had already raised her children and there were so many other things she wanted to do that she had no desire to raise someone else's. So she decided that prophetic dreams were not reliable. However, the dances were fun and they did take her mind off her problems, at least for the evening, so she kept on going to them. Within a couple of weeks of that episode, she met Robert De Young. Bob was energetic and intelligent, fun to talk with, an excellent dancer, and a lover of old cars. He thought old cars had personality and were much nicer than the new cars coming out of Detroit. He would consider it a privilege to drive Mother's Firebird. After all, it was one of the first four-cylinder cars with an overhead camshaft, obviously an exciting car.

Robert De Young, the man who came to mean a great deal to all of us, came over to my grandparents' home to visit Mother that last summer before I went to college. Larry was home for the summer, and after seeing the two of them together, we both agreed that Bob and Mother were well matched. By then we had mostly forgotten our dreams of having our mother marry a man who owned a swimming pool. Larry and I both liked the way Mother and Bob enjoyed each other's company. He was good looking and had a nice sense of humor, and he acted as though he liked our mother a lot. He came from Beaver Falls, Pennsylvania. Living in Texas for a long time, he had acquired some of that deep Texas accent that can make a man sound romantic to someone who has lived in the Northeast all her life.

They had met at a singles dance on July 4, 1969. This was right after she had sold the house. While they danced, Bob was able to guess the sort of foods she liked. He bet she was one of those people who liked to drink scotch, liked her steak cooked rare, and preferred her salad with Roquefort dressing.

"How did you know so much about me?"

"I just observe things. This is the message I get that this is what you like."

Yes, yes, yes, she did like those things. Bob may have been describing what he liked when he guessed her food preferences. He and my mother made a wonderful couple. Mother found an interesting man who could hold an intelligent conversation for hours, and as a bonus he was a great dancer.

Bob never took his first dates out to expensive restaurants, at least not the first time. After their first dance, he took Mother to a waffle house. Mother used to say that they stayed up talking all night. Bob insisted that he did get her home in good time. In any event, Mother was excited. Here was a man with the initials D and Y, as predicted in her dream, and she could get along with him. Both of them had raised their families, and neither was interested in having any more children. Mother and I had been spending the summer in my grandparents' tiny house. Larry was with us for those few months, and that little house was crowded. Mother's life was more than busy. She did not have time for a flirtation that could not go anywhere, and she most certainly did not have time to be hurt again. Bob was intrigued. Her attitude must have aroused his hunting instincts. He took her out for a few more dates and impressed her with his ability to judge people and with his sense of humor.

Mother had been going through the furniture from the house to figure out what she would use in the condominium in Pittsburgh and what she would give away. When Bob came over, Mother was in the midst of reupholstering the dining room chairs and living room couch.

Larry and I were hanging out, not doing a whole lot. Bob stepped out of his car and called over, "I can help you with that. You'll find that I know a little about everything and not a whole lot about anything, you know." As it turned out, he was good at doing many things. He liked working with his hands.

They saw each other nearly every day, and within very few weeks, they started talking about getting married. Bob had done a little research, looking to see which cities across the country would be most likely to have work that he could do as a chemical engineer. He told our mother that business was good down in Houston, Texas. He liked Atlanta and Denver, but he was more familiar with Houston, and his sister lived there as well. He courted Mother with the idea that "We can both do what we want, live together, and if it doesn't work out, you can just go back to Pennsylvania, and what have we lost?" He was the sort of fellow who talked as though he liked to keep the back door open on any relationship so that if it became too uncomfortable he could walk out.

They continued to see each other regularly, and he enjoyed the fact that she was witty, talented, and interested in many different things. Here was a woman who would never be boring. He told her to check out job opportunities in Hawaii as well as some other cities. Bob had a trailer that he could hitch to the back of his car, and in that way he could travel just about anywhere that he wanted to go. Before he had met Mother, he had worked at a number of contract jobs, helping to support his children, who were still in high school, and saving some money for himself along the way.

They played golf together that summer. It never had been Bob's favorite game. He liked to play tennis, so he taught Mother how to play as well. They both enjoyed getting out together, and their competitions were friendly and evenly matched. Once, when they were out playing golf together, they were caught in a rainstorm. We have all seen golfers so dedicated to the game they would not come in out of the rain. Bob and Mother took shelter under a large old tree until the worst of the rain had passed, and then they resumed their game. Both Bob and Mother cherished the memory of that afternoon.

They did consider living and traveling together. At least they talked about doing this, but neither of them believed such relationships worked out well. Mother told Bob, "I can't just go off traveling with a man like this after just six weeks. I have my principles." When she told him that, he asked her whether she would consider marrying him.

"Yes, I would do that," Mother replied.

"We should talk about this," he said.

A few days later Helen called her mother from work and told her she might be getting married. Of course, word spread throughout the office, and by the end of the day, everyone knew. Bob contacted her later, saying, "I thought we were going to talk about this first."

"Well, we did."

She called Rev. Richard Morledge and asked him whether he would be willing to marry her and Bob. He said he would have to meet her intended first. Bob was a Presbyterian, which made Mother feel better, because, as she put it, she didn't want to marry anything odd. When they met, Reverend Morledge told Bob what a fine person my mother was and that he would be marrying into an excellent family. Bob had thought about the sorts of things he wanted to say, so that the minister would approve of him. He hadn't realized that Reverend Morledge had known and respected Helen for a number of years, and he was not entirely certain how he should present himself. It appears obvious, from everything he did after he and my mother were married, that he really was ready to settle down.

However, Reverend Morledge was a careful sort of man. He did not want to officiate at a wedding unless he was certain that the prospective husband and wife were well suited to each other and that they would be a family together. At first, Bob did not appear to be right for our mother, especially as they had known each other for only a few short weeks. He must have interviewed Bob at least four times before he decided to officiate at their wedding. But one thing became clear to both Reverend Morledge and Helen: for all Bob's talk of maintaining his independence, he really did care about her. On Friday, September 26, 1969, exactly twelve weeks after Mother and Bob had met, they were married.

My brother, Larry, wanted to go to the wedding. My grandmother said, "Oh yes, I want to come too." I took a bus home from college so that I could be there. The bus dropped me off right at the door of the church. We were all there when the minister pronounced my mother and Bob man and wife.

It had been a very short courtship. Bob always said that he didn't know he was marrying a grandmother until they were standing on the steps of the courthouse together (getting the marriage license). Their wedding went as well as such impromptu gatherings can be expected to go, except that Bob was upset. Helen had not invited his mother to the wedding. She told me he talked about this gaff on her part for at least two years, regardless of her explanation that she hadn't invited anyone to the wedding. Her family had decided to be there, and she had not been about to stop them. I am not certain Bob felt as badly about this as Mother had thought. I never heard about it.

They chose to spend their honeymoon in Niagara Falls, at the time the honeymoon capital of North America. The two weeks they spent there was an adventure for both of them. Almost as soon as they arrived, Bob came down with the flu. Even the bright pink heart-shaped tub in their hotel room did not soothe his constantly runny nose. He must have felt utterly miserable and told Helen all about it in detail. When I saw her again, she told me she'd had no idea what she had got herself into. According to Bob, she could have walked out of their marriage then and had it annulled, perhaps. She chose to stay with him, and this meant far more to him than anything else she might have done.

When they returned from Niagara Falls, the two of them stayed in Pittsburgh only long enough for Mother to get those last-minute details together and say her good-byes before they went to Houston.

Everything Bob owned was packed in the trailer hitched to his car before they left Pittsburgh. That trailer was his home on wheels, his passport to independence. Mother had narrowed all her possessions down to the few things that could fit in the secondhand '67 Pontiac Firebird she had bought. All she had were her clothes and a guitar, which she had learned to play a few years before meeting Bob. She gave away all her furniture to Uncle Dan and Grandma Gordon. Bob hitched the trailer to his car, and she followed him all the way down to Houston in hers. If you think in terms of Jack Kerouac's *On the Road*, you have a fairly good idea of the sort of adventure they had. They drove down, following the Appalachian Mountains, sleeping overnight at campsites along the way. One night they searched for hours, trying to find the campsite where they had planned to stay. Either the directions they had were vague or the turnoff they needed to find in the midst of the woods was invisible in the dark. They drove back and forth through the woods until they were thoroughly lost. Mother must have been frustrated, but I never heard about that from her. Bob saw a lighted area. It was an electric substation surrounded by a chain-link fence. It wasn't much, but at least there was room to park the trailer. That was where they spent the night. The next morning a police officer who wanted to know what they were doing there awakened them. And yes, they had better move on, and quickly at that. Bob took it all as simply another day's (or night's) work. Mother? I won't even guess how she felt about that.

When they arrived in Houston, Bob found a trailer park that was fairly close to where his sister lived, as well as being in the midst of Houston, close to the Astrodome near Main Street. Mother spent a few weeks thinking about her options. There were a few large department stores, such as Dillard's and Foley's, where she was certain she could get a job as a sales clerk if worse came to worst. In the meantime, she wasn't quite ready to leave off honeymooning. She had not had a real vacation since she had begun working. It felt good to spend a few weeks getting acclimated to Houston and living with Bob. He may have had to show her how he liked his laundry done. "Put the white things here and the black things there." It had been at least ten years since Mother had used a Laundromat. At home it was Kathy and I who took the clothes to the Laundromat, and she used to joke about needing to be taught over again how things like that worked.

She introduced herself to her neighbors in the trailer park and experimented with cooking. Preparing the soufflés and gourmet dinners she had made kept her busy for a few days, until Bob said he wanted something real to eat. He was hungry for pot roasts and potatoes.

"No, no, no," he told her one evening. "This is what I want. It isn't fancy, but it fills the belly."

He proceeded to teach her how to make what she called *slumgullion*. His version of this classic dish was to put a pound of ground meat into a frying pan with a couple of chopped onions and some salt and pepper. When everything was cooked through, he stirred in a can of cream of mushroom soup. When the mess was hot and bubbly, he ladled on top of toasted bread. In the army they called it shit-on-a-shingle, and it filled the men well enough to keep them marching. I don't know whether she served red wine or white with that dish, but she always referred to it as Bob's favorite meal.

Larry came home on leave from the navy during Christmas of 1969. He and I both traveled to Houston to visit our mother for Christmas that year. She and Bob were still living in the little trailer. Larry stayed overnight in a motel on Main Street, while I slept on the couch in the trailer. It was a nice camper trailer for one or two people, but it was never meant to hold more than that. Sitting down to Christmas dinner was an exercise in taking up as little space as possible. We had to climb over built-in cabinets and duck our heads to avoid hitting them on overhead cupboards. Mother was happier than I had seen her for the last several years.

Read a *Greensheet* to Buy

WITHIN A FEW SHORT DAYS, Larry had to go back to his ship and I had to return to school, so I didn't see what went on after Christmas that year. I know that Mother and Bob talked about what she wanted to do. Mother told me that she had been thinking of possibly running an art gallery, or an advertising agency, or an advertising paper like the *Greensheet*, which she had run for Milt Hammond. Any of these things would have been interesting and satisfying.

Bob must not have been irrevocably angry with her for not inviting his mother to their wedding, as soon after New Year's Day he gave her a gift of ten thousand dollars to establish her own version of the *Greensheet*. This was half the money he had been able to save over several years. The gift came as a complete surprise to her.

She told me later that she had no idea Bob had been able to save that much money. Mother had always been a fairly methodical person. She liked to make lists of the things she would need to collect and do whenever she took on a new project. Once she had that money, Mother moved so quickly it was as though her lists had been cooking at the top of her head for a long time. Whatever other pros and cons she may have seen in each of the other business ideas she had entertained, an advertising tabloid was the one she knew best, the one she knew could make money. Besides, it included nearly all the skills that she enjoyed using every day.

As Bob described it, within a week, Helen found office space on the Southwest Freeway between Kirby and Buffalo Speedway, from which she immediately set to work. It may not have been quite as fast as it looked to Bob. Helen's plans were thorough. Besides, all her experiences had been leading up to this moment.

Establishing a successful advertising tabloid involves doing several things at once. In order to attract customers who might be interested in buying space to advertise in such a paper, you must have a sample to show them. The presentation of the paper must be attractive so that people will be interested in looking at the ads. This means making a mockup sheet, seeded with some legitimate ads. These were free ads that she had offered to some of the businesses near her office. Helen created a headline for the front page in large capitals: "Buy a Newspaper to Read," "Read a *Greensheet* to Buy," and at the top right corner, "FREE." The mockup had to look really good, as it was one of her main selling points when she went around to local businesses to solicit their ads.

Before she could go to any of those businesses with her mockup, she had to know which stores and businesses would be willing to give the paper away from their establishments so that customers could pick it up without having to pay for it. She made the mockup, typing those first ads herself. She made dozens and dozens of phone calls, and she spent hours traveling around in order to meet the businessmen she would be dealing with.

At first blush, ten thousand dollars might appear to be a fair amount of money, but when you consider the cost of starting a business—renting office space and purchasing supplies and equipment—you realize how that entire sum could have disappeared within a day or two. The cost of getting her paper printed and out to the stores, where it could be picked up by possible consumers, all had to be factored from that first ten thousand dollars, and everything had to be done with an eye toward immediately bringing in enough money to keep the paper running. For Helen this was a gamble, a bet she was making with herself that everything she had learned at the advertising agencies she had worked for would serve her well in Houston. She gambled that by the end of the first month she would have made enough money to be able to continue working through the second month. To make that ten thousand back, she would have to sell more than fourteen hundred ads, and to keep her business going at a profit she would have to sell several times that, every week.

In Helen's words, business began with the one-inch ad for small businesses. The ad was one column wide, one inch down, with their advertisement in bold type and artwork, versus the local paper's line ads. She sold this one-inch ad for $4.10. All commercial businesses were charged by the inch for advertising space. It called attention to what she planned to do. The paper was free to pick up and read; however, it cost ten cents per word to list furniture, cars, real estate, and other miscellaneous items. She also understood that people do not want to have to travel long distances to buy what they need, unless they are looking for something unique to a specific area. The best she could offer the local businesses was to saturate the local area with their ads. Each specific area would have to be covered at least as well as the daily papers that covered that area. This sort of saturation costs money.

She decided to call her advertising paper the *Greensheet* and print it on green paper. Mother made a call to her previous employer Milt Hammond, owner of the Pittsburgh *Greensheet*, discussed her ideas, and politely told him she was using the name *Greensheet* for her paper. He gave his blessing, and I'm sure they discussed her business plan. Milt's *Greensheet* was filled with editorials along with the advertising. Mother decided to use cartoons and good artwork to fill in around the advertising, along with a write-in advice column called By Cracky. Renato Deaca was the person who created the humorous cartoons and would answer the write-in questions from the readers, making it a fun paper to read, making people laugh while looking through the want ads.

By March 4, 1970, her first paper was ready to go to press. Bob met her after he was finished with his day at work and the two of them dashed to the printers to meet the shop's deadline that evening. This shop was in Channelview, at least a forty-minute drive through Houston, and every second was important, as they had to get those painstakingly prepared galleys to the printer's before it closed.

Houston is a densely populated city. Helen began with the

southwest area, which was where she and Bob were living. Within a few months, she was printing and distributing forty thousand papers every week to that area. Even with the unending work Helen did those first years, there was almost no profit. However, she described that time as not only trying but satisfying and even exhilarating. "I thought it would be a great success, because I was willing to work at it until it became one."

It wasn't easy those first years, pushing every penny that came in back into her business so that she would have enough to buy a piece of expensive equipment or hire someone to sell some more ads. She was distributing her paper in the 7-Elevens and local grocery stores and selling ad space by the cartload. Every week she and Bob would worry whether the mail would arrive on time with the checks, so they would be able to pay for the printer and the help they had hired. If it was a federal holiday and the post office was closed, everyone worried. Somehow, Helen always met her payroll.

Helen's father died June 10, 1970. My grandfather had been ill for a number of years, and my grandmother had dealt with the brunt of his care. Mother took off one week to go to the funeral and left me with the keys to the office. Kathy was in California, so she was able to fly in to attend. Larry was out at sea. I stayed behind in Houston to watch over the office. Grandma continued to live alone in the house my grandfather had built, while my mother worked down in Houston to make her paper a success. I know that her father's death saddened her. She had many good memories of him. However, her first concern was her paper, to get her ads in and get the paper out. Each week she had to sell more ads than she had the week before. Nearly every waking moment of her life was taken up with that paper. She thought it, she ate it, and when she was asleep, she dreamed *Greensheet*.

We forget what it was like to precisely format pages with columns and pictures before computers were available. In 1970, it wasn't possible to sit down at your computer, arrange everything the way you wanted it to be, save it to disk in a PDF file, and take it to the printer to have copies made. Creating columns of text marching down both sides of each page was a painstaking job. The Hammond

Typewriter Company had invented the Varitypcr to do this sort of work. Essentially a glorified mechanical typewriter, it could be compelled to do almost everything a computer word processor does now, as long as you had the time and the patience to figure out how to make it work. It also helped if your fingers were made of cast iron, as you had to pound the keys hard to get them to respond. Lines often had to be typed twice over to position them where you wanted them to be. Helen must have struggled with that machine, as the first person she hired was a secretary who knew how to use it. Over the next few weeks, Helen worked almost around the clock soliciting ads for her paper, until she could afford to hire some salespeople.

The next machines Helen bought were a headliner and a waxer. The headliner does what it says it does. It makes copy in large type that can be cut and pasted onto the page to create headlines. This is where the term cutting and pasting comes from. Now we simply highlight the picture or text we want to move, click a few buttons on the keyboard, and put it where we want it to go. Back then, we literally had to cut the text out from the paper we had typed it onto and paste it onto the sheet aligned and in the position where it was supposed to be in relation to the pictures. After copy was created on the Varityper and the headlines created on the headliner, the pieces were cut from the paper with a utility knife, run through the waxer so that the backs of the individual pieces would be evenly coated with sticky paraffin, and arranged on a full-sized sheet of paper just as they would appear when the paper was printed.

From all the reading she had done years before, Helen understood that if she spent the bit of money that was coming in on herself, she would not be able to spend it on her business to make it grow. As a woman, she was not in a position to get a business loan from any of the local banks. The typical Texas good ol' boy mentality prevailed in Houston in those days, and bank owners would say things like, "We like you, but we can't lend you any money because you are a woman. Now if you would get your husband to cosign it …"

"Absolutely not!" would be her reply. This was her business. Bob had already contributed a lot when he gave her that first ten thousand dollar check and then went on to give her his time. Helen owned this business. From the beginning, it had been her ideas, her know-how, and her energy pushing it forward.

She said not being able to get a loan was a good thing, as it forced her to use only the money she earned to expand her business. This prevented her from having the burden of interest-bearing loans to pay back to a bank at a time when her income was so small that the payments on such a loan would have been painful. That in itself was a large blessing. All the money that the *Greensheet* brought in had to go right back into the company, whether it was to hire another person or two to work for her, or to buy more equipment. One thing she always said was that until her paper consisted of at least twenty-four pages of ads, she could not begin to pay herself for all the time and work she was giving it. Bob used to grow weary of this. He was used to working at jobs where he would be paid regularly for his time. She put most of the money that came in back into the company, letting Bob support her during those first several years. It took five years before Helen was able to take any money for herself from the business.

Bob, who always talked as though he had an eye on the back door, stayed right at her side, even when the only things Helen did were work and sell ads and the only things she talked about were work and selling ads. He helped out in every way he could, even though he may have been peeved that all the work they were doing was not paying back the start-up loan that he had given her. "Not yet" became Helen's mantra. Bob always accepted that Helen knew what she was talking about.

Helen was the first ingredient in her recipe for success. She was a highly intelligent woman, capable of learning most things on the first uptake. The second ingredient in her success was a partner who believed in her and trusted her judgment and ability. Bob was working full-time at another job, and a demanding one at that. Instead of heading home every evening at five o'clock and insisting that Helen be there as well to prepare his supper, he headed over to her office at the end of his day to help with whatever needed to be done. There was always a rush of jobs to get out, and Bob was right there, ready to lend a capable hand. For all the differences in their backgrounds and their outlook on life, the two of them worked well together. Over those early months of their relationship, they developed an understanding and respect for each other that strengthened their marriage, making it possible for Helen to make such a success of the *Greensheet*.

The next ingredient in her success was her family. Not only were Kathy, Larry, and I important to her, but she was important to us. I had stayed up in Pittsburgh for about a year after Mother's marriage, attending Park Point College's School of Nursing. I wanted to see my mother over the holidays, but it was expensive for both Mother and me to have me travel all the way down to Houston and back. A round-trip flight from Pittsburgh to Houston cost about eight hundred dollars, which was a lot of money for us.

When Mother proposed that I move down to Houston, saying that my being there would be less expensive for all of us, I said, "Sure, I'll come down." I missed having her nearby.

She and Bob rented a two-bedroom apartment in a nice neighborhood at the Woodway Square Apartment Complex. She told me that I would have a little space to put my things, and I arranged to fly down to Houston. This was June 4, 1970.

Houston has weather that comes as a shock to anyone who has lived most of her life in the Northeast. Mother met me at the airport, looking neat and proper, as she always did. We hugged, went to get my suitcases, and then headed outside to her car.

Pennsylvania has its share of hot, humid weather, weather that thoroughly enervates even the hardiest people, weather that has the population living there feeling well cooked. Trees surrounded our house in Gibsonia. It was always a few degrees cooler in the woods than it was in town, where the sun's heat is intensified from reflecting on paved surfaces.

When I arrived in Houston, I stepped out of the airport into what felt like a suffocating steam bath. A hundred degrees Fahrenheit with 100 percent humidity are only numbers to the uninitiated. As I said, we went out to the car, the old stick shift Pontiac Firebird that Mother had bought before she and Bob married. It ran fairly well, as she had taken good care of it, but it did not have air-conditioning. You can endure a car without air-conditioning even in some of the warmest weather Pennsylvania has to offer, but it's a different matter entirely in Houston. I sat down in Mother's car and did not question whether my body had turned to liquid and was proceeding to boil away. I knew it had and that the damage would likely be permanent. The car seats burned to touch.

We stopped at a restaurant to have some lunch. This gave Mother a chance to explain what my duties would be in her office. From there we went on to work.

Helen, yes, that was one of the first things she taught me when I started working for her—I was never to call her Mother when I was at work. There she would be known as Helen to her employees, and when we were at work, I was simply one of her employees. She did not want anyone to have the feeling that she had hired me because I was her daughter. She did her best to not give me any breaks that she would not give to anyone else working for her. On top of this, she expected me to be an example to all her other employees. I was expected to do the job as close to perfect as humanly possible. This does not mean that I did not make any mistakes or that I did not spend time struggling to learn how to do the jobs she gave me, and do them well.

By the time I really started working for Helen, she had increased her office space to three rooms, one for the front office, one for the artists and layout people, and one for her salesmen. She had at least three or four salesmen by the time I joined her workforce, and two or three people working on layout. There was enough work in that office to keep every one of us hopping and Helen kept bringing in more work. My first job was to take ads over the phone and do the simple bookkeeping. When on the job, should Helen ask me a question, I must never, ever answer with "I think," and if a customer asked a question I didn't know the answer to, Mother instructed me, "Put them on hold ask me and I will tell you exactly what to say."

She would sit behind her desk with that most supercilious expression on her face. "You think? Don't you know?" I quickly learned that to merely think something was so was too equivocal for proper communication on the job.

Mother would arrive at the office early at seven, allowing time to have a coffee and plan her day. There was a businessman who was a distributor for a new energy drink. He worked the southwest region and had an office down the hall from us. The new energy drink, Gatorade, came in two flavors, orange and lemon, and hit the market in 1969. We called him Mr. Gatorade. He and Mother liked to meet early each morning for coffee and to discuss business. He once remarked, "Running your own business, it's not the pennies you watch, it's the nickels and dimes."

The first time I had to do payroll, I was very disappointed. My name was nowhere on the list of people being paid that week. I had worked hard in Helen's office, harder than some of her other people who were being paid. Didn't I deserve to be paid for all my work? However, Mother had taught Kathy, Larry, and me, from the time we were little, "If you want to cry about it, go to your rooms and cry. Don't do it in front of me." Now, in her business persona as Helen, there was no way I could dare to approach her in tears. I filled out the checks as she had told me to do. It was not until we were driving home that I could raise enough courage to ask her, "Don't I get paid?"

"Yes, of course. Cut yourself a check tomorrow."

She did pay me for a few months. But her paper was still in its infancy, and my check was too much of a drain on the payroll, so after that I worked for room and board and small change. Dressing appropriately for a business office was very important to Helen. She often hired college students to deliver the papers, but they had to come into work dressed in clean pants and button-down shirts, neatly tucked in. Anyone who came in dressed in a pair of blue jeans and a T-shirt would immediately be sent home. I had to wear clean and neatly tailored skirts and blouses, or dresses along with stockings and good shoes.

Ten-hour workdays were normal. Any day we could get out of that office in fewer than ten hours felt like a vacation. The work began to show results very quickly, even though scraping the money together to pay everyone was sometimes a real problem. By the fall of 1970, Helen was again able to move her office space to larger quarters. In the new space, she had a small front room for receiving customers and for classified ads.

It was a year before she could pay me regularly. My first regular paychecks from her were probably about what was the going rate for students. At least I didn't have to ask her for money every time I needed a new pair of stockings.

It felt as though all our lives were totally bound up in that paper.

By the spring of 1971, Helen's customers knew she had a good product. She had to install four phones in her office, connected to a bank with five buttons, and hire several people especially to answer each of the phones. I had the other phone and they were both constantly ringing.

At one point, during 1971, Helen came up fifteen thousand dollars short and could not meet her payroll. She instituted what was then an unorthodox policy. She would not extend credit to her advertisers. "You must now pay for your ads when you order them. I can no longer afford to wait until next month for the check you might send."

Surprised, advertisers would comment, "But none of the other papers charge ahead for their ads!" This was true—none of the other papers charged up front—and it is certainly true that they were dealing with the same problems collecting the fees for their ads as Helen was. However, she was the first owner of that sort of business to have the courage to change a long-standing policy.

"I'm sorry. This is the way *I* have to do business."

The practice of charging for the ad when it is placed is now universal among advertising companies similar to the *Greensheet*.

Even with this change in policy there were still days when at least thirty customers were lined up in the business hallway to get their ads posted in her paper. In part, this was because her paper had hundreds of outlets, so people were sure to find it. She had made it an attractive option for small businessmen advertising their products. And it was reputable. Helen would accept no ads from businesses that had several complaints from customers. People learned to trust her paper.

Greensheet was experiencing phenomenal growth and popularity. One couldn't walk into a convenience store in Houston without seeing the *Greensheet* prominently displayed. Approximately fifty thousand papers were delivered each week. It was marketing genius in its concept, and as a result, it quickly became an established ad paper offering Houstonians an easy, free alternative to scouring the small print line ads in the local newspapers. Another reason for its popularity was the nationwide recession. Houston, being a boomtown, was attracting many people. People needed a paper to find good deals on furniture, cars, and miscellaneous items, as well as painters, remodelers, and other small businesses. Customers were looking for someone local, and the *Greensheet* was the best avenue to find all they wanted.

Greensheet was so successful that another publication tried to duplicate the paper in South Houston area, calling it the *Green Pages*. We received their mail and our customers were confused with this new publication, thinking that it and the *Greensheet* were one and the same. Helen sued them to cease delivery and stop using the name *Green Pages*. The suit was successful, and afterward Helen secured a trademark and copyright for the *Greensheet*. Several years later, another publication tried to start up in Houston called the *Pink Pages*. That paper didn't make it.

Leo Kissner was an attorney Helen met early in her push to establish her business. She appreciated Leo's legal knowledge concerning corporations and small businesses in general. He had helped her through a few legal difficulties, so she invited him to be a member of her board once she was ready to incorporate. She must have done this by the end of 1971, using some of the first profits from the *Greensheet* to do so. Later, in 1983, she invited Dr. Rev. Richard Morledge to be a board member. He and Helen talked about this, and in 1984 he joined the board. Of these two men, Kathy and I used to say that Leo kept Helen and her *Greensheet* safe from legal problems, while Dick kept the moral standards of her company high. She had nine members on her board, most of them businessmen from around the community; however, these two stood out as she had a special friendship with them.

Richard Morledge was at first perplexed when Helen asked him to be a member of her board. "Why do you want a minister on your board? I don't know anything about businesses." Helen wanted him for his ideas and his excellent insight of people. The two of them had got to know each other well many years ago, when she made the giant wreath for his church. While they worked together on that wreath, they talked about philosophy and ethics. They had lively discussions and learned to respect each other's ideas. All right, he agreed to be a member of her board.

Every time Helen needed to hold a meeting, Richard would fly down from Pittsburgh. Helen would meet him at the airport and drive him out to her home, where the two of them would sit up talking into the wee hours of the morning. The following day they would go to the meeting, and afterward they could continue to talk nearly, until it was time for Richard to return to his home in Pittsburgh.

Money Brings Freedom

HELEN DID NOT HAVE A university degree. She was simply a talented woman who read a lot and who analyzed what she read so that she could use it. The one thing that kept her going was the certainty that she knew what it takes to make an advertising company work. She could sell the ads, she could design the paper to put them in, and she could get her paper out where people would find it to buy from it. The one thing that kept her going, and this is probably the most important one, was she always liked being in control of her own destiny, although she would happily learn from other people who knew more than she did. One of her favorite rules was "If you don't know how to do something, then hire someone who can do it for you." But she would never let anyone tell her how she should lead her life. Nor did she want to be dependent on other people who might not work as hard as she did, people who might not feel as deeply committed to making her business work as she was. The other reason that had her hopping up in the morning, after spending long hours at work the night before, was the belief—no, the knowledge—that in our society money brings freedom. With money you are free to get what you want, and perhaps most importantly you are also free to help those people who you would like to help. Helen knew from firsthand experience what it is like to have to scratch for a living. She knew the heartbreak every mother does who cannot provide for her children in the way she would like. She always appreciated how lucky she was in that her mother and her brother stood behind her in her business ventures. She always appreciated the way Bob trusted her business judgment and put his energy into helping her, in very tangible ways. She wanted to give back by building a business that could support her family. As her business grew and she was able to keep herself more than comfortable, she wanted to help other people as well. After all, enough money could solve a lot of problems. Mother liked helping people. She believed strongly that it is up to us to make positive changes in a world that can be anything but just. I believe that she preferred to help people individually, much more than she liked giving to institutions that were presumably established to help needy people.

There was a woman who worked in her office who was trying to get away from her abusive husband. Helen opened her home to this woman to give her a safe place to stay until she could get on her feet. Later, when the *Greensheet* was bringing in more money, she helped a young woman whose situation was particularly awful by helping her to establish a completely different identity at the Dallas *Greensheet*, far from where her husband lived, so that she and her children would be safe. She always felt drawn to helping women who were struggling to make ends meet on their own. A number of such women who came to work for Mother.

My sister Kathy and her husband, Mike Stermon, were struggling in Gibsonia, Pennsylvania, after Mike left the navy. Helen suggested they move to Houston, and she would give him a job working for her company. In the summer of 1972 they arrived in Houston, and Mike joined the *Greensheet* as a salesman.

By this time, Larry was still in the navy, stationed in Scotland, learning about computers and working on a nuclear submarine. Everything he knew and did was classified information. Mother visited Larry in Scotland, and while there, she discovered a nunnery. There she met a sister who enjoyed music and was teaching her students to play the guitar. Unfortunately, the nun had only one guitar for her lessons. When Helen returned to Houston, she put an ad in the *Greensheet*: "Wanted: will buy old guitars for $10.00." Mother collected around fifty guitars and sent them all off to the nunnery for the students there. Mother did those kinds of things for people, people who never asked for her help but needed it.

Constant work, coupled with knowledge and insight and the ability not only to perceive how situations could work out but also to act on what you see, does pay. Patience with the building of the *Greensheet* paid off in 1972. The *Greensheet* increased to twenty-four pages from the four pages she had started with. Helen believed strongly that in order to gain respect from her employees, she had to give them respect in return.

Nineteen seventy-three was not the easiest year for our mother. Surgery could no longer help her to hear. The doctor told her that the condition of her ears was so bad that surgery was like working within a tiny tube filled with oatmeal. She was terrified, although she didn't say much about what she was thinking at that time. Being deaf to the world around you is isolating. People seldom understand the problems deaf people experience. Hearing loss can destroy marriage and friendships and can make it impossible for one to keep a job, let alone run a business that brings in thousands of dollars a day.

Helen was devastated over having to lose her music again and wondered if she would have to give up her business as well. She did have a secretary who could type more than 120 words a minute. She thought that perhaps she could stay in control of things if she had this secretary sit beside her in her office all day, typing out what people said to her so that she could read it and tell them what to do and where to go. It wasn't a perfect solution; life seldom offers perfect solutions. She was determined she would try that, along with any other sorts of aids she could pull together, before she would consent to giving up her business.

Thankfully, both for Mother's sanity as well as that of the people around her, the doctors she saw were able to fit her with hearing aids that enabled her to continue what she loved doing, running her business and making music. Hearing aids were not as well developed back in the early 1970s as they are now. When sitting among a crowd of people, such as in a restaurant, hearing aids do not differentiate between one voice and another, as our ears do when they are fully functional. This must have presented difficulties when she played music with ensembles, as she enjoyed doing. Our mother was so thankful to be able to hear that she never complained about her hearing aids not functioning as she would have liked. She continued to do the things she liked, and with gusto. Medicine and technology seemed to advance as she needed it. As far as Helen was concerned, a pair of hearing aids looped around her ears should not create any more of a stigma than a pair of glasses across her face. She could see no reason why anyone should think any less of her for having to wear them.

No matter how good you are, you will not be able to please everyone all the time, and Helen understood this. Some of her employees saw her as controlling. While Helen did not see herself that way, claiming that she wanted to have control over her own life, while other people should control their lives, on the job it was different. The *Greensheet* was entirely Helen's business, and while she would be interested in listening to anyone's ideas, especially people who presumably knew what they were talking about, she decided how this paper should proceed. She enjoyed telling a group of men, "This is the way it is going to be" and having them get up to do what she said. Oddly, she seldom hired women to take on leadership positions within her company. There may have been a number of good reasons for this, along with some that were purely subconscious on her part. She did, however, hire many women for sales positions, and they had every chance to move up to a leadership position. Every time she did promote a woman to a position of leadership, she would hand her a sizable check and tell her to go out to buy herself some decent clothes for work.

Helen was clear about her expectations for those whom she employed. She expected them to follow her directives to the letter, leaving no room for experimentation with Helen's way. She was clear about how she preferred her employees to dress for the office. Her management style was clear: perform according to her wishes or seek employment elsewhere. Helen knew how to motivate her employees, expressing her will, "Do as I say, and you will be successful." She was also clear about keeping one's personal life out of the office. The workplace was where business was conducted, and employees were to keep the two separate.

By 1973, Helen had moved her offices to the building next door at 2712 Southwest Freeway. The paper had almost literally swallowed me whole. I was no longer in nursing school. I worked full-time for my mother and took some business courses in the evening, except on Tuesday night. Tuesday nights we were at the office until midnight or later, finishing the last ads and making sure the paper was laid out to Helen's specifications. So that we could get it to the pressroom in Channelview on time to have it printed, cut, and folded so that we could distribute it on Thursday morning.

Changing her collection policy enabled Helen to save up for a printing press. By the end of 1973, Helen had saved enough money from her paper to buy her first press. It would be a relief not to have to deal with smudged copy from the print shop, after she had paid for good, clean copy. It would certainly be a relief not to have to deal with an outside print shop's schedule. She did her research and found a secondhand Vanguard press. It was old, even for the early 1970s. Harris Press had bought the Vanguard Company and taken over their product several years before. There was only one gentleman in the continental United States who knew how to operate that press, and he had retired several years before Helen bought it. However, it could print a thirty-two-page paper and it had been manufactured to print the sort of copy she needed. The company had the press refurbished so that it would do what it had been made to do and painted it so that it would look fresh. On the day it arrived and the erector was in the back room putting all its parts together, Helen went to her salesmen to say, "All right. Raise your hand if you know how to take your car engine apart and put it back together." Kathy's husband, Mike Stermon, was the only man who admitted he knew how to do such things to his car.

"Okay, good. You're going to be the pressman. The fellow out there setting it up will show you how it works." Mike went to the back room where the press was being set up and Helen went to her office. As far as she could see, her problem was solved. However, the press demanded a lot. Neither of them enjoyed working on that press. It was old and getting tired. You could say it had personality. Gears and wheels that might have worked smoothly when the press was new were wearing out and not meshing as they should have. No matter how quickly they wanted that machine to run, it would only go so fast. If they tried to push the paper through too quickly, it would rumple up under the rollers and come out hopelessly creased and smeared.

There is sometimes an advantage to working at contract jobs. The man who does this learns how to do a variety of things and learns how to deal with many different situations. This was especially true for Bob. When he and Mike worked on the press, they were able to be creative about solving problems that inevitably came up.

Helen was often back in the press room, trying to push things along so that the paper would get out in time. She would lend a hand whenever the press broke down, which happened nearly every time they ran it. Most of the clothes Helen owned were eventually stained with printer's ink and grease. I clearly remember her coming into the pressroom one afternoon wearing a nice white suit. She had to find out why the job was running so slowly and could not resist getting into the middle of it. Between stacking the freshly printed papers and checking the ink, her suit was white no more. Even with all its foibles, that press did save money for the *Greensheet*.

Never did I think of my mother as the sort of person who would purposely seek out attention—she was too proper for that—but she always loved it when people gave her their attention, and with her years of advertising experience behind her, she understood how important it is to maintain a large presence in people's minds. Her offices were located in a one-story building in southwest Houston. That building fit in very nicely with all the other buildings on the frontage road of Southwest Freeway. At least it did until Helen decided to let people know where she was. She checked with the town hall about the advertising codes for that section of town and then had a *Greensheet* sign erected that was two stories tall. It was lit up so that people could see it from miles around. This way, everyone knew where her *Greensheet* office was located. It changed the look of the frontage road, but Helen was too busy building her business to be concerned about that.

In 1973, when Kathy joined the company, she worked part-time as an assistant bookkeeper and later as full-time head bookkeeper. She knew simple bookkeeping, but now she was in charge of all the bookkeeping, including payroll and taxes. She read books on simple bookkeeping and taxes. It was learn as you go. Helen was a great teacher but very impatient when mistakes were made. In those days, Kathy typed payroll checks on an old typewriter, and she sometimes made mistakes when typing the employees' names. This did not go over well with the employees or with Helen. Kathy recalls the time when she responded to one of Helen's questions with "I think ..."

Helen was quick to correct her. "What do you mean you think? Always know the answers when I ask you!" Kathy never made that mistake again.

Now that Kathy was working full-time and her husband, Mike Stermon, was running the pressroom, Helen was not only managing the company, but she was learning her new role with us—that of employer rather than mother. She was a taskmaster and required us all to know our positions and perform better than anyone else in the company. Helen was patient with us but not tolerant of any mistakes made a second time.

In those days, Kathy and Mike would deliver their children to school and daycare before coming to work. Kathy remembers many times when she would pick the children up in the afternoon and return to work in the evenings while the press was still running and Mike was working late. Helen always stayed until the press run was finished. Kathy and Mother would visit while the children would play in the hallway. Michael and Michelle literally grew up in the hallways of the *Greensheet* amid the building of the business.

Grandma Gordon had been living alone in the little house in Gibsonia ever since Grandpap died five years before. She was getting older, and it wasn't as easy as it had once been for her to take care of herself. Mother and Uncle Dan were concerned over how Grandma would manage alone in that little house in the winter months. Even with Uncle Dan next door he was still concerned for her. None of us had either the time or the money to travel back and forth to make sure she was all right, so in 1974, Mother invited her to join us in Houston.

I am not certain how our grandmother felt about making that trip. Houston was far away from Pittsburgh, and she would miss her church friends. Besides, she and her husband had planned to live in that little cabin until the day they died. I imagine that this move must have been one of the great adventures of her life. Her son Dan and his wife, Mabel, helped her pack up those things she wanted to have with her, and they either gave away or sold everything else, including the house. Uncle Dan and Aunt Mabel drove her remaining items to Houston. Mother found an apartment in Treemont Retirement Community off Westheimer, where she could live nearby and still be independent. We all enjoyed the fact that my grandmother was there, the family would make appointments with Grandma to visit as she became very busy living there. It did not take long for Grandmother to get used to her new living arrangements. Being in a new city, there were many things she liked almost right away. Meeting new people and going to fine restaurants was a great adventure compared to her country life in Gibsonia. I do know that when she came to the office to see what we were doing there, she was very impressed with Helen's business sense, the way her daughter dealt with bankers and businessmen in general and kept her employees motivated to work hard for her.

Every Thursday, without fail, Mother would have a driver pick up Grandma, and the two would spend the afternoon together in Mother's office. Mother gave her the job of counting the change and rolling it. She would sometimes sit and knit or crochet while Helen carried on the business of the day. Even during interviews, there was Grandma sitting off to the side counting change. At all the parties and functions, Grandma was always in attendance.

This was our grandmother, who knew well how to deal with doctors when she saw they might be doing something questionable or detrimental to one of her patients—she woman who knew how to keep the nurses and aids on her floor hopping so that everything ran efficiently and who was loved and respected by everyone who worked with her. She was the woman who was always known to her associates as Gentle Grace. One almost envisions the proverbial iron hand inside the velvet glove. In truth, she would do nearly anything for her friends, as long as she believed it would be good for them. Our mother felt as though praise from Grandma Gordon was high praise indeed.

In 1975, Leo Kissner found a building he thought would be ideal for Helen's operation, the Allen Parkway Building. He offered to purchase a sixteenth part of it, believing that whatever happened with Helen's business, his share would be worth the expense. Helen took a look at the building. It did need work. There were places where the roof leaked. The space was arranged so that everyone would be more comfortable than we had been once the building had been repaired. A few tenants were conducting their businesses from there at the time of the sale. If they would only stay until after she had closed on the building and was ready to move her business into it, the rent they paid would be a big help. The tenants remained there for a year after *Greensheet* moved in. I am certain she thought about Leo paying for a sixteenth of the building, but knowing my mother, I cannot imagine she considered it very long. She went to Leo to say no. She did not want any partners. It was her business and that was the way she would keep it.

Helen bought the building at 3701 Allen Parkway, and a warehouse behind it on Terrell Street. Again, she did not go to the banks; she had saved enough money to buy the building without a loan. The property was a bargain at the time, approximately $500,000. This building came to mean a lot to all of us. We spent so much time there it was almost like home, and we only went back to our apartments to sleep. It was a good move for the *Greensheet*. The space where our offices had been located was noisy. That elderly Vanguard press had been right next door to the rooms where we answered the telephones, making it difficult to carry out conversations. Even so, we had so many customers calling us that we needed to have at least ten people to operate the phones at all times. The layout people and the artists often wore earplugs to deaden the sound of the press rattling and banging away in the next room, but nobody else could do that. Anyone who has ever walked through the pressroom of a large newspaper knows how loud those presses can be. It takes perseverance and patience of a high order to work with that racket behind you all day. The new layout at Allan Parkway permitted us to put the press in its own building.

The purchase of this building was a tangible sign that Helen was beginning to earn the kind of money that she had always dreamed of earning. Allen Parkway was a two-story building with about fifteen thousand square feet of working space and another twelve thousand square feet of storage room for the press on Terrell Street, behind the building.

Helen had plans to purchase a newer Harris press, although it too was used, and sell the old Vanguard before the move to the Allen Parkway Building. Helen had been running an ad in the *Greensheet* to sell the old press, but there had not been many inquiries about it. First, the *Greensheet* did not usually advertise such expensive items. If she could, she would get enough from the sale of the old press to cover the cost of the new one. The old Vanguard had cost about thirty thousand dollars. She had managed to pay for the loan with Harris Press in full within six months, establishing credit with Harris Press. Most people who saw her ad didn't need a press that big, if they were interested in owning one at all, or if they wanted such a piece of equipment, they would not have looked for it in the *Greensheet*. Then the Mexicans came.

They said they had the money and they insisted they would pay Helen before they moved the press from the building on 2712 Southwest Freeway. They said they wanted it to print a revolutionary paper down in Chihuahua, Mexico, but if they declared it as a press when they crossed the border, they would have to pay high duty fees on it. They proceeded to take the machine apart, this press that Bob and Mike had been keeping in as fine condition as they could, and beat and scraped the paint off of it. They were going to claim it as scrap metal. They spent a few days doing this to each piece before they loaded it onto their truck. It was a big old flatbed truck that swayed so much under the weight of that press, which it looked as though it would collapse before they got everything back to their home base. I believe everyone in the office began to wonder about the honesty of those men. Bob's suspicions were definitely aroused. He and Helen decided they had better hire someone to spend the night in the warehouse so that those men would not drive out with the press during the wee hours of the morning. Helen paid one of the young men who was a press helper, Burt Woodall, to spend a few nights in the warehouse, just to keep an eye on what was going on and protect the press.

At last, the Mexicans had everything loaded onto their truck and were starting to back it out of the building with only paying for half the amount agreed upon. Bob hopped onto the top of the back of the truck and shouted, "Wait a minute. You guys don't pay for this press, this truck ain't going nowhere!"

"It's not all there. We are not paying for incomplete inventory," their spokesman shouted back.

"We'll do an inventory now," Bob said.

Helen called the police, believing that a few men in blue with their badges prominently displayed might help bring order to the situation. Bob spent the next several hours going through every item on the inventory, in order to make certain everything was on the truck. Once they had established that the Mexicans had the entire press, two of them went off somewhere—no one bothered to ask where—to get the money.

We learned later that the fellow who bought the press had been on the losing side of the revolution. He was shot and never heard from again. We were never able to find out what happened to the old press, or even whether they had been able to get it set up and working again. However, the fifty thousand dollars Helen received from them gave her a very tidy down payment for her new press. The Harris press was already set up in the new location on Terrell Street behind the Allen Parkway Building.

I thought this was all quite an adventure, an introduction to a sort of reality that I had never seen before and would not likely see again, at least not close up like that. To Helen, it was all in a day's work. As far as she was concerned, some people are simply crazy and you have to be able to deal with it. If you are not capable of handling weirdness like that, you're not ready to lead a corporation.

Helen could now afford to hire an experienced press operator, to the relief of Mike Stermon. They hired Joe Mancia. As it turned out, he was a press helper who in the early days left the *Greensheet* to gain experience to become a press operator. Joe Mancia found out we were looking for a new press operator and applied for the job. Helen hired him, and he remained the pressman until his untimely and sudden death in 2011. He was a loyal, sincere, and hardworking man.

I believe that Helen always saw the work that she did as her way of making a difference in the world, at least where her family was concerned. Helen and her brother Dan had always been close. They looked out for each other. In his own way, Dan also deeply cared about his family. Both he and Helen may have felt little need to make many friends beyond their family.

Uncle Dan came down from Gibsonia to help with the repairs on the building. His work was always excellent. He was the sort of craftsman who would take the time to do the job right. He'd been a carpenter all his life and could not think of himself as doing any other sort of work. The mill where he had worked, both with his father and his brother-in-law, was closing, and it is likely that he and Helen spoke of opening a mill or a furniture company, where he could work down in Houston if he and Mabel wanted to move there. He was not quite ready to retire, and everyone who knew him agreed it would be good if he could continue working, at least for a few more years.

Helen established the *Southland Furniture Company* in 1977. In the beginning, they started with quality millwork and specialty design woodwork. However, Bob and Uncle Dan soon realized that specialty jobs like mill working were not in high demand. Then Bob designed a line of knockdown furniture, what is now called DIY, or do it yourself, and Dan was in charge of a crew of workmen manufacturing the unassembled pieces to sell. Helen changed the name of the company to Gordon Furniture, and they continued building knock down furniture such as bookcases and desks, which they sold to Lowes, Home Depot, and other hardware stores. Our cousins Bill Gordon and George Hacke also worked with the company. When family was able and willing to do the work, Helen would hire them first. When Uncle Dan retired to travel the country in his mobile home in 1989, Helen closed the shop down. Uncle Dan had worked there for Helen, and Helen kept the business going for Uncle Dan. It was not making a huge profit, and they were both done with the woodworking business. "What's done is done and away with it all" was Helen's opinion. She commissioned Bob to sell all the equipment.

Helen met Barbara Harding, a corporate handwriting analyst, during the late 1970s. Ms. Harding had been studying handwriting for years and could tell very quickly whether someone was likely to be dishonest or have a difficult time dealing with stress, merely by analyzing their handwriting. Helen herself was a good judge of character, although she never considered herself the sort of person who would sit down to analyze a situation to figure out why it was running in a given direction. She liked to act, push, prod, and lead; however, she treated employees that she liked with a great deal of respect. She strongly believed that if you want people to respect you, you must earn that respect by treating them respectfully. Helen did not always behave the way she preached. On the other hand, Barbara was an analyst. She understood what sorts of characters worked well in a large organization. Most of her insights were absolutely right, and Helen respected this.

For a few years, Helen was sending packets of handwriting samples up to Boston for Barbara to analyze, a few times a week, and they talked together over the phone nearly every day. She was perhaps one of the closest friends Helen had during that time, aside from Bob and her children. Helen believed that before hiring a person, it was crucial to understand whether that person was driven to earn a lot of money or whether he preferred to work on a project until it had been done to the best of his ability. Most of us fall somewhere between those ends of that continuum. The first set of people, the ones who believed work was not worth doing unless they could make a lot of money, Helen would hire as salesmen. She would often hire people who had no experience doing this, telling the prospective employee, "I'm going to make an excellent salesman of you." If that person learned quickly and was willing to follow her rules all the way through, they did turn out to be good salesmen. She was right; it is often easier to start fresh, teaching someone how you want him to function on the job, than it is to undo training that has already been done. The second set of people, the ones who were essentially artisans and wanted to be able to take pride in the work they did, she usually hired as secretaries or layout artists.

Sometime in 1976, Helen hired a young college graduate, Bob's son-in-law, Mike Bergdahl, to be the first personnel director at the *Greensheet*. This was Mike's first job out of college, and he took this opportunity seriously. He made it a point to work with all the managers and to work in each department so he could understand what kind of personnel he should be hiring. There were now approximately two hundred employees. At last Helen could finally delegate the hiring to someone else. Mike did all the hiring for all the departments, but Helen had the final say on managers and salespeople. The *Greensheet* was growing very quickly, and there was a constant need for new classified sales personnel and a high turnover in the pressroom. After Mike left the *Greensheet*, he worked for a variety of companies, and he is currently an author and motivational speaker. When I asked Mike for an interview of his insights on Helen for this book, he thoughtfully gave me his impressions, and I would like to share them as he wrote them.

This is what he has to say about his experiences working for Helen:

* * *

Insights from Helen
Michael Bergdahl, *Greensheet's* First Human Resources Director

On Believing in People

When I graduated from college, Helen hired me to work at the *Greensheet* as her first HR director. It didn't matter to Helen that I had minimal experience or qualifications for the job. She believed in my work ethic and my ability to learn and that was enough.

At that time, the biggest challenge we faced was hiring the staff for the sales departments, and keeping the pressroom schedules filled with press help. The challenges we faced to retain press helpers was daunting. Turnover of employees was high, the work was hard, and the heat and humidity made it difficult to hold on to our employees. Helen was always supportive and provided encouragement when at times I was a bit demoralized by how difficult it was to keep the pressroom staffed. She had walked in my shoes, and she knew how tough it was because she had done the hiring herself up until just before I arrived! The fact is she had done all the jobs in the company at one time or another when she was starting out.

Leadership lesson: When a leader delegates responsibility to inexperienced people, they will do whatever it takes to get the job done, to prove to that leader that they were equal to the challenge.

On Perseverance

In the 1970s it was a miracle we were able to get the *Greensheet* published and out into the market each week! Helen was the master motivator even when we were late on deadlines—which seemed like most of the time! The sales department would often turn in ad copy late, the composing room would then be late putting the pages together, the plates would be late arriving in the pressroom, and the presses would be behind schedule. I remember we would often load delivery trucks directly from bundles of papers coming off the press.

The ink was literally still wet! Each week the same deadline related scenarios played out, and to me it seemed almost miraculously that we would get the papers published.

Helen really liked the publishing business. She handled the pressures of all the deadlines with grace and firm leadership. Sure, she would get flustered and angry at times with the missed deadlines, but when the going got tough, she was a great leader. I swear she had both ink and ice running through her veins simultaneously.

Leadership lesson: When you're missing deadlines, fatigue sets in, and it is critical that leaders demand commitment from everyone on the team until the job is finished.

On Getting Things Done

During the paper shortages of the 1970s, we were desperate to have enough paper to print the *Greensheet*. We would use whatever kind of paper available. We printed with yellow paper, pink paper, green paper, and white paper. Sometimes we even had to combine colors in the same edition for lack of paper! One day Helen and I were in her office and we saw a paper delivery truck arrive to deliver paper to the pressroom warehouse. A few minutes later, we saw the same truck pulling away without having offloaded its precious cargo of paper rolls. The truck stopped at the stop sign in front of the Allen Parkway office in view of Helen's office and she and I ran out the door to stop the truck before it had a chance to leave to deliver those paper rolls to one of the daily papers in Houston, which were also in desperate need of paper. Fortunately, the traffic on Allen Parkway was heavy that morning, and we were successful in catching that truck and turning it around to deliver that load of paper to the *Greensheet*. As it turns out, our press operators had told the driver they could not stop the printing presses to unload the truck, and the driver refused to leave the trailer so we could unload it later. To my surprise, Helen directed me to unload the truck. I told her I didn't know how to run the clamp truck (fork truck) to unload the paper rolls. She told me it was easy to learn and now was a good time. So I drove that clamp truck in a three-piece suit and tie and unloaded that truckload of paper rolls in ninety-five-degree heat and high humidity. I was soaking wet with sweat when I finished but we got the paper.

Leadership lesson: In a small entrepreneurial business, there are times when you have to throw out the rule book, take risks, roll up your sleeves, and just do whatever it takes to get the job done.

On Having Courage in Your Convictions

Steve Inskeep was the head of finance and accounting in the early days of *Greesheet*. One day he and I were in Helen's office (at her request for security) as she argued with the father of an employee who had just been terminated for violating a company policy. The exchange became heated between the two of them, and Steve and I were forced to stand between them to prevent a boxing match from erupting. Picture Steve and I face-to-face with Helen on one side of us and that irate father on the other, both of them screaming at each and getting close to exchanging blows. Finally, Helen had had enough. She demanded that Steve and I physically remove the irate father from her office! She yelled, "Throw him out; throw him out!" Steve and I looked at each other, and without hesitation each of us grabbed the father by a shoulder. As Helen opened the door to the sidewalk, we pushed him out the door, and Steve, I, and the terminated employee's father ended up in a heap on the ground on the sidewalk. Helen managed to have the last word while standing in the doorway.

Leadership lesson: As an entrepreneur or business leader you have to make tough decisions. Some of those decisions are popular and some are not, but business is not a democracy. When a business leader makes a difficult decision, it almost always comes with some degree of financial or even legal risk, but Helen believed you should do what you know is right and never be afraid to deal with any issue head-on because of those perceived risks.

* * *

I never knew Helen to be unable to defend either herself or the things she believed were important in her life. She knew how to speak in order to get things done, and if she had to be tough, or if she lost her temper in the process, she saw it as part of what was necessary to defend her business. On the other hand, her values were traditional. She always had a strong sense of propriety. There were certain things one simply does not talk about. If Kathy and I were in a public place with her, such as a restaurant, and for whatever reason one of us felt the need to cry, instead of being sympathetic, Mother would hiss at her offending daughter, "For heaven's sake, go to the women's room, wash your face, and take some aspirin. And don't come back until you are under control."

This does not mean that she could not empathize with people who were sick or in trouble. But that is as far as it went; she had no patience for crying, tantrums, or emotional outbursts from employees or family. However, there were times when she had to be restrained from verbally attacking some hapless offending employee or delivery person. "I don't care. I want him out of here." You could see the steam rising from Helen's head. The fellow may have asked a question that she thought was redundant, or perhaps she simply didn't like the look on his face. Whatever it was this fellow had done was the spark that lit the fuse. If neither Kathy nor I or any of her other more trusted employees could calm her down, we would have to let the fellow go and spend time and money to hire and teach someone else to do his job.

These are the sorts of things that add color to a personality. On the other hand, they illustrate the fact that she was never afraid to say what she believed, or to do what she saw as necessary to get the job done. And it illustrates that one of my mother's greatest strengths was also a weakness.

The people working for Helen had to do what she said and in the way she said it. It was her business, and she believed her ideas would work. If she wanted them to sell in a certain way or dress in a certain way, they were free to do it her way or not work for her. Helen did not care about their personal lives. Yes, she did care about them as people, but personal lives are separate from their business life.

Helen's management style was distinctive in that she was able to lead people with respect. But she did it her way. Employees wanted to work for her and learn from her, and Helen was able to convince you that you would be great, and she was going to make you do it. She understood how to get people to do what she wanted, even when they did not want to. Helen many times dismissed people who were not willing to do as she instructed them to do. "Do as I say and you will be successful." If they were not on that same thinking or did not impress Helen, she would dismiss them. At times she was harsh with new employees that did not rally to her way. On to the next candidate.

Once, when I asked my mother what character traits she had that she believed had made her such a good businesswoman, she described a few incidents that had occurred in her office that I did not remember. Some of them were rather scary. She said that there were times when some of her employees would get into fights with each other, and sometimes they were rather violent about it. She remembered at least two times when someone brought in a gun. Her response was to act calmly, the way a good teacher would when a young child brings in a dangerous toy. "Give it to me and I will take care of it until it's time for you to go home." She would then tell them that if they did not straighten up she would have to let them go.

As a businesswoman, she could not afford to care whether an employee straightened up. He could be replaced. She could become emotionally involved with the outcome, and in any event, she knew just how she would treat the situation, so she was always confident, no matter what sort of craziness might be happening. On a personal level, Helen wanted people to pull themselves together, behave reasonably, and do the job she had hired them to do. However, from a business perspective it did not matter; she knew she could deal with them.

During our regular family gatherings we would discuss those crazy situations, the employment problems, and the challenges facing the *Greensheet*. We all lived and breathed the *Greensheet* until the early '80s, when Bob declared, "Enough of the *Greensheet* discussions.

We need new topics." For Helen it was not difficult at all, because she was a great conversationalist who could go on for hours about a wide range of topics. Inevitably, problems at the *Greensheet* would arise that naturally required Helen's attention during our family gatherings. Eventually, we all learned to leave the business at the office and enjoy our family time together.

In the late '70s, Mother began researching the use of computers to do the composition work, classified ads, as well as the headliner. In 1978, Larry joined the company. His first task was to identify which computer system we needed and the company that could best serve our needs. Larry had been trained in computer languages while in the navy, so he recommended we go with a system by a company known as Tel-Star. Unfortunately, it took months for the composition department to get online. When it came time to move on to the classified department, the company did not fulfill their contract. In 1980, Helen filed a lawsuit against the Tel-Star for failing to finish the job for which they were hired, causing the *Greenshee*t to lose money. It took until 1983 for the case to get to court, and our attorney, Leo Kissner, represented us once again. Although Helen won the case and received stock in the company, Tel-Star went out of business, making her stock worthless.

In those days, computer systems were very expensive. Helen knew she would need help from a bank to obtain the money to purchase such a system for the *Greensheet*. The first banker she approached told her, "Helen, you think you are like everyone else doing business in Houston, but you are not. You are a woman, and we just can't loan women money."

"I need a loan to move my company along more quickly," she explained. "I can use my company as collateral, but I need the money to buy a $700,000 computer system." The banks would not loan her the money. That was how women were treated throughout most of the '70s.

Finally, she met Walter Johnson, who worked for Bank of the Southwest. He seemed willing to give Helen a chance. He made an appointment to meet with her at her place of business. When he arrived at the *Greensheet*, he brought along an officer of the bank. In order to receive the loan, Helen had to agree to do all her banking at his bank. While discussing the $700,000 loan, a large truck rolled up in front of Helen's office window. Her office on the Allen Parkway had ten-foot floor-to-ceiling windows, giving her an excellent view of the Tel-Star truck unloading huge pieces of computer equipment. Walter Johnson asked, "Oh, is that the computer? How did you know we were going to give you the money?"

"Well, Walter, if you weren't going to give me the money, I'd have to go somewhere else."

Johnson told her he rarely met anyone with that much confidence, so he decided to give her the loan. As a result, Helen remained loyal to Walter Johnson and the Bank of the Southwest for many years. Helen Gordon was the first woman ever allowed into the elite bank's dining room for the bankers and their customers. It had been a man's realm until she became their customer, and Walter proudly told her that she was the first woman he had ever hosted in the exclusive space. It was rather a feather in her cap, although I don't believe she ate there very often, as she was more than busy running her business. As the familiar phrase goes, banks never want to loan money when you need it, but when you don't need money, they seem to be giving it away. Suddenly, the banks were soliciting Helen. I'm sure she appreciated the irony.

The two computers by the Tel-Star Computer System was so massive that it required at least five hundred square feet of office space. They seemed to have a life of their own. Helen decided to hold a "Name the Computer" contest within the company. As a result, Frick and Frack were born. There were two other machines that received data from Frick and Frack, so Larry named them Ping and Pong. The Headliner machine and countless typewriters were suddenly obsolete. Another new machine, the pyrofax, eliminated the tedious process of paper to camera to negative to plate process.

The *Greensheet* was thriving in the Houston area, so Helen began to look at the demographics of other cities. She decided to expand the *Greensheet* and chose Austin for her first venture. In 1977, Austin had one edition in circulation. The next year, she opened the Dallas office with two editions, and in 1983 she expanded to San Antonio with three editions. These were all sales offices. They sold the product, flew the ad copy to Houston for printing, and then a driver would deliver the printed publication to each city for distribution and delivery. The composition room now worked every day from 8:00 a.m. until 2:00 a.m. the next day, or until the paper went to the pressroom.

Dan and Helen elementary years.

Helen and Verne.

Allen Pkwy. building. Hurricane Alicia ripped out the front windows.

Bill Chaney back for his second round with Greensheet.

Ted Stiles and Clay Parks

Mr. Gatorade

Larry and Rebecca

Mike Stermon and Rebecca

Kathy, Grandma, Rebecca and Helen

Kathy, Helen and Rebecca

Renato wrapped in ribbon.
Herb Taylor.

Kathy, Grandma and Laura Cahill

The trucks with a different elf on each one.

Helen Gordon, below, owner and publisher of the Greensheet, has a green-tinged mansion in La Porte overlooking Galveston Bay. It includes a pool house next to a waterfall-fed pool, right, and well-manicured Japanese, herb and rose gardens.

Larry Reese Photos / Chronicle

The color of money

Gordon enjoying this green-house effect

By BILL DISESSA
Houston Chronicle

GREEN truly is the color of success for Helen Gordon.

The 49-year-old founder of the Greensheet has built a fortune and a green-tinged mansion from the profits of the weekly shopper that saturates Houston after starting on a shoestring nearly two decades ago.

As a struggling painter trained in commercial art, Gordon sold her house in Pittsburgh for $13,000 and used the meager venture capital to play a prophetic marketing hunch. Houston's Sun Belt economy was ripe for a free weekly tabloid of classified advertisements for a growing tide of rummage-sale junkies, antiques collectors and used home, car and appliance buyers.

With two assistants and a leased press, Gordon founded the Greensheet in 1970, coining the name from the unusual color of its paper. In those days, it only could be found on the city's Southwest side. Now, the Greensheet has more than 1,000 individual distribution points in greater Houston.

"Looking back, it was ridiculous," Gordon said of her whimsical move from Pittsburgh and her early toehold here.

Today, green has turned gold for the Greensheet's owner and publisher, who relishes her privacy in a secluded 14,000-square-foot home that would make Lifestyles of the Rich and Famous' Robin Leach green with envy.

Overlooking Galveston Bay in La Porte's affluent Crescent Shores subdivision along Highway 146, the two-story green-tinged exterior is viewed by some as an eccentric tribute to Gordon's wealth.

Janie Bais, spokeswoman for the city of La Porte, said many passers-by associate what actually is Pennsylvania bluestone with the Greensheet.

"They think it's her signature," said Bais. She notes that others mistake Gordon's nine-hole golf

See GREEN on Page 8D.

Houston Chronicle - October 13, 1988

1982
Helen and Larry

1982
Helen and Bob dancing

1983
Dan and Helen at his wedding

1983 The family at Dan's second wedding

1986
Helen dancing with her step-son Brian DeYoung

1986
Helen, Mike and Sherlyl Bergdahl, Brian DeYoung, and Bob

Dr. Morledge and Helen

1991
Helen with great nephew and adopted son Justin Gordon

1991
Rebecca and Helen

1991
Helen and Kathy

Barbara Harding, Bob & Helen

Bob and Helen on a cruise sometime in the 1990's

2000 Kathy, Helen, Bob

30th Anniversary for the Greensheet

Helen and Bob 2009

Helen with her great nephew and adopted son, Justin Gordon

Gibsonia, a house Helen and Verne built

Tamarack, La Porte, Texas

Helen and Bob's home on Sunset Blvd., Houston, Texas

Stirring the Pot

THE 1970S HAD BEEN MOTHER'S decade to establish the basic things that were supremely important to her—her relationship with her husband, Bob; the *Greensheet*, which was truly her bequest to all her children; and the evolving relationship with her children, working with her on the *Greensheet*. The eighties was the decade she became a businesswoman to be reckoned with in Houston.

Computers were just beginning to come into their own. They were as large as a small truck and needed to be kept in temperature- and humidity-controlled glass-walled rooms. Those were the days when rows of secretaries were hired to type reams of data cards, and it could take most of a day to feed the information into the computer in order to get the desired output. Very few people understood how computers worked. Programming languages were just beginning to be written by teams of bright young men. As a communications and computer specialist, Larry had several lucrative job offers immediately after leaving the navy in 1978.

Mother wanted all her children to work with her as she built up her business, as she envisioned that they would one day own it. She sent Larry an offer, which essentially said, "If you come work for me, I'll pay you more than what any of the other companies are offering." I believe Larry and his wife would have come down to Houston even if Helen could not have met the other companies' best offer. Within a few weeks, he and his new family were established in an apartment of their own in Houston, and Larry was hard at work on the computer system in Helen's office.

That offbeat sense of humor he had shown as a youngster was

well developed by the time he came to work for Helen. He knew how to make people in almost any situation laugh, and he knew how to be everyone's friend. He would patiently sit down with his coworkers to show them how they could do their jobs better, offering his insights and helping them build up their self-confidence. He managed the computer and pressroom for several years, capitalizing on at least some of the training he had received in the navy as a communications and computer expert.

At home, things were not quite so easy. The last few months of my grandmother's life were bittersweet. She began to have problems with dementia and needed to be reminded what medications she should take on each day. She was also in and out of the hospital with heart problems. Her doctor described the probable course her dementia would follow, and she realized it wasn't long before she needed help with nearly all aspects of daily living. Grandma asked Mother if she could move with Bob and Mother in their townhouse. As a nurse, she knew she needed more care and did not want to die alone in her apartment. At that time, Mother and Bob had a comfortable townhouse with two upstairs guestrooms. Mother arranged the larger bedroom for Grandma so that she would have everything she needed. Mother had a housekeeper, Alma, who would stay with our grandmother during the day while we were all at work. This way she could keep an eye on everything that happened far better than she could, had her mother been in a nursing home.

Mother and Grandma had always been close, and knowing how much Mother enjoyed talking about ideas, I am certain the two of them regularly sat up talking whenever they could, although I doubt they had many late nights, as Grandma usually went to bed around nine in the evening. Eventually our grandmother could no longer hold her own in such conversations. Mother made sure my grandmother was able to die peacefully in her bed. I know that my grandmother appreciated all the care Mother gave her, even though she no longer truly understood what was happening around her. I recall Mother coming downstairs, brokenhearted. She had just been sitting with our grandmother when Grandma had said, "I wish Helen would visit more often."

As short-term memory disappears, the victim tends to recede into the life they led in the past, in Grandma's case a young woman with growing children. She therefore failed to recognize those children as adults with children of their own. Our grandmother died in her sleep October 4, 1979.

Helen had opened our Dallas office back in 1977, and she asked if I would like to be the general manager. She had begun telling me I should move out there to take it over. I had not wanted to run an office by myself until I felt confident that I understood every aspect of the business. However, by 1980, I had been working for Helen for ten years. She announced one day that I did understand everything I needed in order to run an office for her, so she was sending me out to run her Dallas office. I was ready to go. She really wanted someone she could trust to do what she told them to do. It truth, by 1980, my confidence was strong, and I looked forward to moving out to Dallas. I liked being around my mother. I had only been away from Mother when I was in school for the year I was in Point Park College. For several months, I traveled back and forth to Houston nearly every other weekend, just to stay grounded and to reassure myself that everything was all right. I stayed with Mother and Bob on those trips, and they were always happy to see me.

Over the years, Helen had written and refined her training manual. It was the bible I used when I trained our salespeople, and by the time I left for Dallas, I had memorized it. One of Helen's most important orders was to make certain everyone dresses appropriately. This helps to create a businesslike atmosphere so that when clients walk in they expect that their needs will be handled in a competent manner. No one who knew Helen then will ever forget the time she chased a young man down the hallway, fire extinguisher in hand, shouting at him, "You will wear a tie when you come to work here!" he never showed up in her office again without a necktie.

The linchpin of her business, her salespeople had to be on the ball. Each commercial salesperson in her employ had to make at least fifty phone calls every day. The individual classified ads were constantly being called in by phone. The commercial ads was were the biggest part of the pie. The success of the *Greensheet* depends on maintaining an increase of the commercial ads. Just because they made a few good sales the day before, the salespeople were not permitted to rest their laurels. Everyone in the office must keep moving, keep producing. Most importantly, I had to establish my plan of action and train my people to follow it. If my people were not trained to jump when I told them, I would have problems.

Listing those rules makes everything sound simple. Helen always used to tell me, "If you don't know what to do, ask me. But if you have any brains, you can figure it out for yourself." In other words, *Go stand on your own two feet*. I was glad that she felt confident in my ability.

I liked running the Dallas office, once I got used to the differences in routine. In Houston, I had been running the composition department, working days and nights. It was an adjustment being at work by eight in the morning rather than ten, as I had in Houston, and only working until five in the afternoon on most days, rather than midnight or later, as we all had in composition department in Houston.

In Houston, I had become quite skilled at hiring and training sales staff. This can be rather ticklish, because if the person I hired did not work out, I would have to get rid of that person within three months. If I did not, and the employee either could not or would not do the job well after that three-month period, I would have to deal with a pile of legal considerations in order to get rid of them. Sometimes I felt like a heel, having to tell someone I would not be keeping him or her when it was obvious they wanted the job and had been trying to do it well. It was just that they had not succeeded in doing it the way we needed in order to make the *Greensheet* successful. The responsibility is nerve wracking, and I could understand my mother's nearly complete separation of her business life from her personal life. The stress of the responsibility was one reason I flew back to Houston so frequently. I needed the reassurance, even if it was only subliminal, that I was doing the right things.

Bob and Helen were beginning to feel that they should slow

down. They had been talking for a long time about building a house, a retreat where they could go on weekends. It would be nice if it were near the bay so that Bob could go boating. He had imagined a little A-frame house with a deck all around it and a couple of bedrooms inside. It would be an informal space where they could, as she put it, kick their feet off and relax, perhaps with a friend or two or their grandchildren. Ideally, it would be a simple place where they could get away from the office and all its demands, and it would be small, a place where they could stop for a few hours to smell the flowers before heading back to Houston and work on Monday morning. To this end, they bought a piece of oceanfront property in San Leon, Texas.

When they first considered property for their vacation house, Bob did not bargain on Helen's philosophy of life. Helen, who could no more imagine being truly contented with something small and inexpensive than eat dirt, could not let plans for such a modest vacation home come to fruition as long as she had a choice. Now that her *Greensheet* was thriving, she certainly did have a choice. Bob should have realized this as soon as she hired an architect to design their little A-frame. The drawings wouldn't even fit on their San Leon property, let alone the house Helen envisioned. Helen was determined that this would be a house in which she could entertain her family and friends in the style that she had always dreamed of being accustomed to. The house she and her architect designed boasted well over fourteen thousand square feet of living space, only three or four times larger than the average luxury home.

Studies have shown that people who feel powerless find large, expensive items much more attractive than smaller, less ostentatious ones. When I think about what my mother was like when I was growing up, and the stories she and her mother used to tell us of the years when she was a little girl, it is difficult for me to imagine my mother ever really feeling powerless, although at times this may have been the case. Everyone in her family worked hard in order to maintain a middle-class standard of living. Her father had a fine intellect, but he also had his share of weaknesses. Her parents did encourage their children to earn pennies, nickels, and dimes by doing chores around the house and selling lemonade from a stand in their front yard, as well as washing her father's car. Poverty is a very real problem, but one tends to experience it as relative in terms of what he has experienced before and to how his friends and neighbors are living. I can imagine my grandparents telling her, "You cannot squeeze blood from a stone," whenever she or her brother wanted something that presumably children from other families had.

Helen became obsessed with amassing money when she was a little girl. No child wants to grow up to be so poor that he cannot lead a dignified and useful life, and Helen fixated on the idea that money granted the power to take care of herself and the people she loved. It only took a few words from the first architect they saw to convince her that as long as they were building a house, they should build the house that she really wanted.

Bob and Helen searched for several months for a property where they could put this dream house, before settling on a three-acre lot in La Porte, Texas. There were wonderful views all around from this piece of property, and the architect's plans would make it the grandest dwelling in the area by far. Bob enjoyed working with Helen to make their dream vacation home as beautiful as they could. As he explained it, the two of them had an agreement. For instance, if Helen wanted something that seemed truly outlandish to Bob, all he had to do was say so, and that would be the end of it. In addition, the same was true for Helen—if Bob wanted to do something that she did not believe would work, she simply put her foot down, and that was that.

The plans for this house included a master bedroom with two baths, one for him and one for her, nine guest rooms each with a private bath, and a living room that was so large ordinary furniture would be lost in it. The main floor had floor-to-ceiling plate glass windows that looked out onto their property and beyond to the bay. Mother designed an art studio upstairs from their bedroom. The music room with her grand piano looked out over the pool and rose garden.

She planned the house on such a grand scale that it had to be reduced in size by 10 percent in order to fit on the property. She and Bob would later buy the two properties on either side of theirs, making a total of nine acres and giving Helen enough space to have a nine-hole golf course landscaped around the house, as well as an Olympic-size swimming pool.

Helen's sister-in-law Mabel died in 1981. She was only forty-six at the time, too young to be dying. Even thought their life choices had been very different, she and my mother had shared many things. Mabel had been our mother's steady companion when she first wrestled with her hearing loss, sitting by her nearly every day through that most difficult time in her life, patiently helping her to learn how to read lips. Uncle Dan was devastated by her death. Except for his sister, Mabel was the only person who truly understood him.

In those days, doctors did not understand the way women respond to heart attacks as well as they did men, mainly because women were not included in heart attack studies. Uncle Danny had already had a double bypass operation not too long before, and Aunt Mabel did not want to say or do anything that would upset him. Uncle Danny was going out for a walk, and Aunt Mabel was feeling tired and uncomfortable. Instead of going for a walk with him, she lay down on the couch to take a nap while he was out. The last thing our uncle heard her say was, "Bye, Danny," as he headed out the door. By the time he returned, she was dead. It was February 14, 1981, Valentine's Day, and it would from thereafter be a day of mourning for Uncle Dan.

Both Helen's parents were now gone. This meant that Helen was now the oldest member of her family. She was, in effect, the matriarch. I suspect she felt the rest of the family would be depending on her to hold things together. In order to do this well she needed, more than ever, her business to be successful.

In the winter of 1981, Helen sent Larry to run the Chicago office. Allison Chittock from the Dallas office went there as manager of sales and Larry manager of the pressroom and distribution. Within six months, Allison left and Larry became general manager of the whole operation. He had six neighborhood editions of the paper to oversee, and he put a tremendous amount of work into that. We didn't call it the *Greensheet* in Illinois, because another company was already using that name, so we called it the *Ad Paper* instead.

The years I spent in Dallas were a lot of fun, although there were some hair-raising moments. This may be because newspaper work attracts people who are artistic and dramatic and who like to express themselves in, shall we say, unorthodox ways. I had employees who were either too fearful or too disdainful of coming to me to help work things out with the other employees, and so they would take revenge into their own hands, creating disruptions that I could spend pages describing.

One incident stands out above all the others. For at least ten years, the *Greensheet* had been taping all phone calls for training purposes. The phone company had shown us how to do this, and it was fast becoming policy among all businesses. Because these recordings are so ubiquitous, and because we play them back to our employees as examples of good and not-so-good ways to handle phone calls, we assumed that all our employees knew that those recordings were being made. We would even ask them, "Do you want to be taped today?"

One employee, who shall remain nameless, was very angry about something, about what I do not remember. He made an appointment with the local district attorney's office to storm our Dallas office on a day when Helen was scheduled to be there. Helen had called us at eight in the morning to say she would not be able to make it down that day. So she missed the first part of the fun. At eight thirty that morning, a string of large black cars surrounded our building. Men in black suits, I didn't count how many but enough to swarm into the building and guard all the entrances and exits, proceeded to cut all the wires to our phones. Their leader informed me that we were being charged with illegal phone tapping. They sequestered all the managers in the main conference room, and I had to beg them to permit me to make one phone call to Helen so that she could call a lawyer.

Helen immediately saw to it that every phone in all her offices had a label put on it stating that conversations would be taped and that anyone using that phone would automatically be giving his consent to be taped. Even so, our business in Dallas came to a standstill. All our employees in that city were subpoenaed to appear before the grand jury about the phone tapping. It didn't take long to figure out who had gone to the district attorney's office. He had intended to put the *Greensheet* out of business and he was proud of what he had accomplished. I couldn't fire him, and I couldn't even reprimand him, as much as I really wanted to give him a piece of my mind. Either would have been considered "tampering with a witness."

I felt awful. Helen paced the floor of her office, knowing there wasn't anything she could do about the situation in Dallas. After about eight months of waiting, Helen and I had our turns to testify before the district attorney. As we were walking into the office, Helen told me to sit quiet and not say anything. She swept into that office like a monarch. In her husky, well-modulated voice, she explained to the assistant DA that on the day they are hired, all of our employees give their consent to have their conversations taped. She described in detail the changes in policy she had made concerning use of the phones as soon as this situation had arisen. Then, waving her charm like a flag—Grace Kelly had nothing over Helen—she told the fellow she was a mere woman doing what she could to run a successful business. The assistant DA was enthralled. Within half an hour, he had dropped all the charges.

I loved being in charge of the office and being able to run the show as I thought best, with no one peering over my shoulder. I trained several sales representatives, who, as of this writing, are still working from our Dallas office and doing very well. As our income increased, I would add one or two more employees. Once a month, I flew back to Houston, making a day trip of it, leaving Dallas during the wee hours of the morning and landing in Houston in time to attend the meeting with Helen, my sister, and the other branch managers, and then flying back to Dallas in the afternoon. It was not a pace that permitted me to turn around, think, contemplate, or philosophize. However, there is a definite joy in accomplishment.

Helen worked constantly to expand her kingdom. She would not permit her *Greensheet* to do anything but expand. She used meetings to lay down the law, saying, "This is what I want you to accomplish, and this is how I expect you will do it." In addition to these meetings, Helen made regular trips to each of her branch offices to make sure that the work was progressing as she had specified.

We printed all the papers from all the branch offices in Houston. Each city had the ad copy ready by the deadline and had it flown to Houston on the Southwest Airlines carrier service. Two days later, the printed *Greensheet* would be trucked back, ready to distribute.

Helen frequently found projects that appeared to look good for her business, and her judgment was excellent. It may not have appeared that way to many of the people who worked with her, but Helen did sit down to analyze the pros and cons of pushing a new project through or doing things a certain way. She taught Kathy, Larry, and I to sit down with a piece of paper to list the good things that could happen if we chose a certain plan of action. Then we were to list the bad things, those things that could go wrong with such a project. Benjamin Franklin explained that one should spend a couple of days making his list, as ideas often take a few days to gel in one's mind. Then he said, and Mother taught us, one should add up both sides of the list to see whether the benefits outweighed the cons.

Once she had come to a conclusion, Helen liked to push her projects through, making adjustments as she went along. She was generally able to understand the overall picture very quickly and felt that time spent planning the small things was wasted. She believed it was far too easy to get lost in the planning and fail to get anything done. I like to see all our little buttons lined up in a row before we jump pell-mell into a project. "But Helen," I would say, "this would work a whole lot better if we knew what ..." describing what I believed was essential to the project.

Helen, in her most proper manner, would say, "I have heard your ideas, but I am going to conduct it my way," and she would invariably go off to do what she had originally set out to do. She did take all the suggestions given to her and would sometimes combine them with her ideas. This had always been the way Helen operated, and some authorities list it among the chief characteristics of successful entrepreneurs. As far as Helen was concerned, only one person should be in charge of a business office, and as long as it was her business, she would definitely be that person.

Helen bought the building at 2601 Main Street in Houston in 1983. There were tenants on most of the floors when she bought it, except for the third floor. Once that space was remodeled, Kathy moved the sales offices there. The remaining departments of *Greensheet* stayed at the Allen Parkway Building. Kathy was in charge of all the display ads in the Houston *Greensheet*, as well as collecting rent from the tenants who were still on the first and second floors. It was Kathy's responsibility to tell them that the *Greensheet* would not renew their leases when they ended.

Kathy very quickly learned how to stand up for what she believed was right when dealing with Helen. It wasn't long before she was saying things like, "Well, if I'm going to be in charge of that department, you will have to stay out of it." Kathy was not the fireball our mother was. She liked to carefully plan what the people under her would be expected to do before she told them what she would need. As with many people who know what they want and like to be totally in charge of certain aspects of their lives, Helen respected others who show a similar need to be in control. While Kathy thoroughly understood what it means to compromise—after all, she had been the peacekeeper between Larry and me when we were children.

As the tenants vacated our new building, the first floor became the classified ads and human resource offices and the second floor held the composition department. The fourth floor became the accounting department and the fifth floor ultimately held Helen's office, a receptionist area, and a conference room. Even with Helen in the same building, Kathy managed to maintain her independence from Helen's business leadership.

As her business interests expanded, Helen had to delegate more responsibilities. In the 1970s, this began with delegating specific processes to people who were more skilled than she was at doing those things. By the 1980s, she had *Greensheet* offices in Dallas, Fort Worth, Chicago, San Antonio, and Austin. She had to trust that the people running those offices were bringing in the best results possible. Still, no matter how far flung her offices were—and her idea was that she would eventually have *Greensheet* offices in every major city across the country—it was hard for Helen to give up her sense of control. No matter whose leadership philosophy she might experiment with, deep down she always believed that one person had to be in charge in order for things to run smoothly.

In the early 1980s, Dr. Edwards Deming made a reputation for himself in Japan as an advisor to corporate management teams. Helen, the avid reader, found that Dr. Demings's books provided a new perspective on business. His books distilled his ideas on corporate management into fourteen points, such as creating consistency of purpose and building quality into the product at all levels so that inspectors would not be needed. He spoke of driving out fear so that people could work effectively, and he emphasized substituting leadership for management and quotas. It must be remembered that no matter what bright-eyed system of management one chooses to use in a corporate setting, personality is the defining element. An office is shaped not only by the personalities of its leaders but also by the personalities of the workers. In most instances, personality has a stronger influence on the way the office runs than whatever system the management chooses. From the time Helen was a child, she was too independent to be anything but a dictator. No matter what ideas were in vogue, Helen would use them to suit her purposes. She understood that a dictator could be benevolent and generous, but she could not permit anyone but herself to be in charge of her domain.

On another level, Helen liked to do what she called "stirring the pot." It kept people on their toes and kept the mood in her office rather edgy at times. For example, Dr. Deming advocated that employees should be part of the decision-making process. After reading his books, Helen inaugurated companywide meetings where she announced that workers in all departments could do what they wanted and have a say in their pay. This very definitely stirred the pot, and the ensuing pandemonium might have been entertaining as long as you didn't have to deal with it. I suspect Dr. Deming would have had a few interesting things to say had he known what Helen did in his name.

Kathy had very carefully worked out what her sales employees should earn. Now the people in her department were clamoring to know why they could not have more money and why they could not run the department as they chose. Kathy had to spend the next few weeks disillusioning her employees of this misinformation in order to get things running smoothly again. She had to tell Helen to please stay out of the departments she ran. I suspect Helen derived a perverse sort of enjoyment over the fracas she created, nearly as much as she enjoyed keeping everyone under her benevolent thumb.

In 1982, Helen hired route coordinators to verify her paper deliveries. The coordinators followed the delivery vans to all the stores and business establishments where the paper was distributed to make sure the new edition of the paper had been left in the bins assigned to it and the old editions had been cleared away. He would go into each store and talk with the owner to make sure that the young men who were delivering the papers came in when they were supposed to, made the pickups and deliveries as had been agreed upon, and were courteous to the store owner and his employees. He also stopped at other stores along the way to talk with the proprietors about having the *Greensheet* distributed from their stores. This was part of the process of having the paper's circulation legally verified, a process that newspapers had been doing for many years. Helen's *Greensheet* was the first free paper to have this done. It was a way to make her paper legitimate in the eyes of the public and other businesspeople.

Mr. Green

A S HELEN'S BUSINESS GREW, HER hiring practice became more involved. Barbara Harding's handwriting analyses had always been helpful, and she continued to depend on Barbara when screening potential managers. By the early 1980s, Helen needed people who could handle larger amounts of responsibility, as well as stress. She began to give personality tests and polygraph tests, in addition to having Barbara Harding's analysis, to each applicant who came looking for a high-level position in her company. She had to know how well suited they were to the job, and she needed to know whether they were honest. With the expansions, Helen hoped to realize, she would need a chief financial officer. For this she placed an ad in the *Wall Street Journal*. Bill Cheney applied, and he proved to be an excellent officer in her company.

Every manager has his own style, his own way to deal with employees. Helen's style was essentially "This is what I want. Listen up, because I'm not explaining it again." Once she had given her explanation, she expected people to behave intelligently and jump into the project. Bill had to get used to her managerial style, but he learned quickly. He always found it best if he kept his reports to her short, a page or two at most, rounding most of the numbers up to the nearest thousand. While on the job, each learned to understand and appreciate how the other worked. Socially, they shared an interest in tennis. Bill and his wife, Nikki, often played doubles with Bob and Helen. Bill and Helen usually partnered in those matches, and their friendship grew.

I met Mike Blakeley while I was in Dallas in February 1982. After meeting through mutual friends, Mike showed interest in working at the *Greensheet*. He came to my office to apply for work as a sales manager. When I sat down to interview him, I found him to be charming and fun. I said to him, "If I hire you, I wouldn't be able to go out on another date with you, and I really do want to get to know you."

He said he would like to work for me and date me. I said he could take the personality tests, the polygraph tests, and the handwriting analysis, and we would see. When the results came back, I called him to and told him, "I have good news and I have bad news for you. The good news is that you passed the tests very nicely. The bad news is that I really want to get to know you."

We were so enamored of each other that we began talking about getting married within a few months after we met. Mother and Bob had made their decision to get married very quickly after they met, and their relationship tended to be a good one. Yes, they had some disagreements—it would be impossible for two strong minded people to live together and not have any—but they were good for each other. Bob was proud of Helen's business sense, and Helen opened up a world and a way of life for Bob that he never would have had otherwise. I believed that Mike and I would be good for each other as well.

When I told Mother we were getting married, she enthusiastically arranged a beautiful wedding for us. If she had not been running the *Greensheet*, she probably could have made a lot of money as an event planner. She knew how to get people organized and keep them excited so that the project would go off beautifully. With flowers, guests, photographers, caterers, and a wedding gown to drool over, it was a memorable event, and for a few years Mike Blakeley and I were happy together.

Meanwhile Helen continued full steam ahead with her business, and the building of her house, Tamarack, as we called it, continued. The first structure to go up was a magnificent A-frame pool house with a wraparound deck. The design for this must have been in honor of Bob's wish for an A-frame getaway. My sister and I used to bring our children and spend weekends there. Bob and Helen made a wonderful pair of grandparents. Where our mother may have appeared to be a little brusque, perhaps a little off-putting, Bob enjoyed playing with our children, making up stories and teasing them. From that wraparound porch, we watched as that tremendous house was built. If I had been interested in learning how to construct a building, I could have watched the construction crew and learned quite a bit. One month the foundation was dug and blocked. I remember walking around its perimeter. It wasn't quite as large as a football stadium, but you could have played a tidy game of baseball down in that hole. As a little girl I would have made that excavated hole be my stage and danced from one end to the other. Another month the frame began to go up, and if the foundation had appeared to be vast, we marveled over the proportions outlined by that frame. It could have been a house for giants. After the first few times, though, the novelty wore off. This was simply Mother's home. That house represented who and what she had been so determined to make of herself during those years when Kathy, Larry, and I were growing up.

Bob and Helen took their first vacation outside the United States in 1983. That summer the two of them traveled up to Montreal, Canada, in order to take a much needed break from the routine and the stress of the *Greensheet*. News on the television and frantic phone calls to and from Houston brought Helen immediately back down to her office. Hurricane Alicia had hit the coast, cutting a swath of devastation from the Gulf of Mexico through a number of cities and hitting Houston on August 18. It was the most destructive storm that had hit the city in years, as well as the most dramatic. Gale-force winds blew out windows in many of the downtown skyscrapers. Tree branches and live power lines fell from the poles and blocked most of the streets. And of course there was flooding. It was estimated that this storm caused more than $2 billion in damage. In 2011 dollars, this would be well over $5 billion. So many windows were smashed due to flying debris blown from rooftops that the city council changed the coding for roof construction in order to prevent that from happening again. More than two thousand homes were destroyed in Houston.

With power lines down and families needing to be taken care of as much as the businesses, few people went to work that day, although everyone who worked for Helen knew that her first priority was keeping the *Greensheet* rolling. Ted Stiles had been working as a route coordinator for about a year. It was a position of responsibility and he had handled it well. Ted was one of those few who made it to work. Phone lines in our office and all over town were dysfunctional. Some places had no phone service at all. We were lucky in that the few people who made it to work that day could receive calls in our pressroom and could make calls from our main office. This was not the most practical arrangement, but it was better than nothing. It meant that someone had to race back and forth, up and down the street between the pressroom and the office, through floodwater, wind, and rain every step of the way. When a call came in, Ted would take the message and then hike down the block to the office to Helen with the information. This went on for a couple of hours. Helen told him to pull a few hundred dollars out of the cash drawer and to go around to see if he could find a crew of power people and convince them to turn on the power to our press room, as our generators were burned out. He was successful with that.

Most of the businessmen in downtown Houston closed down until working conditions could be brought back more or less to normal, but Helen wasn't that kind of businessperson. Her paper would go out no matter what. Within a day, she had her crew of employees cleaning up the damage and rolling with the next paper. No matter what else happened, her *Greensheet* would survive to triumph. The *Greensheet* was delivered to all the businesses that were open. Many businesses lost so much that they had to pack up and leave Houston, or close down altogether.

After the hurricane, Helen felt a sense of trust in Ted. He had carried the office during the emergency, making sure that she knew everything important that was going on. The woman who had been working for Helen as her personal secretary would soon be leaving, and I am certain Helen did consider hiring and training someone else to fill that position. I am also certain that she considered moving one of the other people who were working in her office to fill that position. She had a few professional people on her staff, and at least one or two of them could have worked out. She liked the way Ted Stiles had taken charge during the hurricane, immediately stepping in to turn a situation around that could have been a disaster and getting the office well on the road to being cleaned up and running again, all the while keeping Helen apprised of what was happening. Though Houston lost a number of its small businesses because of that hurricane, nothing had stopped the *Greensheet*, largely due to Ted Stiles's quick thinking. Helen always respected a person who was good at thinking on his feet. However, as soon as she mentioned Ted's name in conjunction with personal secretary, people piped up with, "No, he won't do. He's not the right sort of person for this position. You want a woman who will project the right image." Her CFO thought it was one of the craziest things Helen could have done. Helen had never been one to let other people tell her what to do. She was so set on doing everything her own way.

She called Ted to her office for an interview. Ted walked in and sat down. Helen eyed him over her coffee cup. "How do you feel about working for a woman?"

Ted confidently eyed he back. "Well, I already do work for a woman. I work for you."

"Good answer." She put down her cup and riffled through some papers on her desk. "How much do you want to get paid?"

"As much as I can get." That was the best answer Ted could have given. Helen had always wanted as much money as she could get, and she admired that trait in other people. The two of them understood each other very well.

Houston's business culture was then, and in many ways still is, based on the good ol' boy network, making it very difficult for women to break in. When most people think of a woman running a business, they think of her doing the sort of work that is traditionally done by women, such as nursing, teaching, sewing, cooking, and secretarial. Even within those professions, men tended to be placed in the top positions. Up until she hired Ted Stiles, clients and customers calling in with complaints were put on the line to Mrs. Green, a fictitious complaint manager. When she first started her business, Helen was Mrs. Green. Even I had been Mrs. Green for a few years, and I knew how nasty some people could be. Many people who called in were rude, insisting that women were not capable of running a business and that they must speak to the real owner, who had to be a man. Ted said he would take the job as long as he would be known as Helen's administrative assistant, rather than her secretary.

Once she put Ted Stiles in charge of being Mr. Green, many businessmen assumed that because he was a man answering to the name of Mr. Green, he must be in charge of the business. Obviously, Mr. Green runs the *Greensheet*, right? A couple of gentlemen from one of the local banks came over to speak with the owner of the *Greensheet* about using their bank's services. They came in for their appointment, walked into Ted's office, and sat down to give him their sales pitch. Ted listened to them for a few minutes before saying, "How stupid can you be? You came to make a sale, but you did not even do enough research to know who your potential customer is."

Helen heard what was happening and told them to come over to her office. Once those two men were again seated, she was brutal. "Why would I risk my money with a company that will not even take the time to find out who it should be talking to?" Those gentlemen left with apologies, and I do not believe we heard from that bank again. The battles she fought convincing other businessmen that she was the real owner of the *Greensheet*, and a highly competent one at that, contributed to her sense that she had to constantly fight in order to maintain control of her business.

Ted discovered that working for Helen was a learning experience on many levels. However, Helen was quick to give instructions and encouragement. "Ted, you can do this. I know you can, it's easy." Working directly for Helen one had to have a strong temperament. If he said point-blank, "This wouldn't be good for the *Greensheet*," Helen listened to his ideas. When it was a good idea, she would adopt it. Still, for all her insistence that her way was the only way to run her business, she always respected her workers' personal space.

Ted recalled one incident that illustrates this. He was driving Helen to an appointment in the car she had bought for him to use. Out of habit, she lit up a cigarette. When she was on the job, Helen smoked a great deal. Mark Twain's comment that he restricted himself to smoking only one cigar at a time, in order to maintain his health, almost fit Helen. She used to light one cigarette from another. Ted was light smoker at the time, but he did not enjoy smoke in the areas where he worked. Even so, he did not feel shy about telling Helen, "I don't permit people to smoke in this car." Once he said it, Helen immediately put her cigarette out and never smoked in his car again.

Helen enjoyed being the first to use new ideas and technology. She was one of the first people in Houston to take advantage of the new technology, a mobile telephone. In the early 1980s, the batteries for these things were so big that you needed a large briefcase just to carry them around. They were not the sort of thing you would talk on while jogging down the street, as we do now. Helen could afford it, and she did use it a few times. It was more private than a pay phone, although when I think about the technology that existed then, I doubt it was as practical as pay phones were. I suspect that she bought it in order to show off. With that device, she could make calls from almost anywhere, although wireless connections were in their infancy and not necessary the most dependable means of communication. Whether or not it was useful, it was definitely a conversation starter.

Many people have asked Kathy and me what it was like to work for our mother. At least some of those people have experienced dysfunctional relationships with their parents and cannot imagine working for them in any sort of business venture. Mother was a strong minded, clear-sighted woman, and we always knew where we stood with her. She was proud of us and what we were able to do, and she would tell us so. Throughout our childhood, she always enjoyed being with us, although she taught us to understand that, after her family, business was the second most important factor in her life. We did have to adjust to dealing with her on the job; however, there were three things we had that anyone new to the *Greensheet* did not. First, we had known Mother all our lives, and we trusted that ultimately she would be reasonable with us. Second, Mother knew us. She knew our strengths and had taught us that we could overcome our weaknesses. Third, as much as she insisted that on the job, her relationship toward us would be no different than it was toward any other employee; she really wanted each of us to be a major part of her business. As long as we would meet her at least halfway, we would be part of the *Greensheet*. However, she would never have put up with any of us on the job if we had consistently messed things up. From long experience, we understood that she would respect our ideas. Besides, Kathy, Larry, and I all wanted to do well. Years later, Mother told me that she always knew her children were smart. She had put us in managerial positions almost from the start, but we had to earn respect do the job well to keep it so that the other employees would not be able to take advantage of us.

Kathy never felt she had to prove herself as a businesswoman to the extent our mother did. By the mid-1980s, there were many professional women, certainly more than there had been when Helen first went into business, so Kathy never felt herself to be as much an anomaly as our mother had. Besides, she had grown up with Mother as her primary example. When Kathy took over, some people missed that sense of excitement Helen had always engendered, as Kathy is a much quieter person. She likes to plan things carefully and she likes to get her workers' opinions before she tells them what she expects them to do. In some ways, her style of leadership is closer to what Dr. Deming taught than Helen's ever was.

Larry had a small heart attack in the fall of 1983. There may have been others, but this one was strong enough to send him to a hospital to be diagnosed. It was not supposed to be the end of the world for him, although he would have to cut back on those things in his life that were creating stress, and of course change his diet. Heart attacks have become so common for executives in our society they are nearly a rite of passage. Larry was her son, and Helen did everything she could to ensure that he would live a long life. Some of the best cardiologists were in Houston. She had him move his family back there, and she put him into a work situation that would be less stressful than the load he had been carrying in Chicago. The Chicago office was a position that carried so many responsibilities it could aggravate anyone's heart condition. He moved his family back to Houston, where he took up the work he had done before, running the computers. Whatever they did, it was not enough. Larry died at ten thirty in the evening of October 18, 1984. He had eaten his dinner and gone to the other room to run the treadmill. When he was finished, he felt unusually tired, so he lay down. Pressure on his chest mounted up, so he told his daughter to get his wife. None of us expected that he would die so young.

A parent should never have to bury her child. The space that child had occupied is filled with crushing emptiness for the parent. Our mother was never quite the same after Larry's death. People who knew her describe her as being quieter and sterner than she had been before. She never wanted to talk about Larry after he died. If anyone mentioned his name in conversation, she would change the subject. Anger, yes. Helen always knew how to express her anger, but sadness, due to pain or loss, was an emotion she seldom had patience for, either in herself or in other people, and I do not believe she ever permitted herself a time of mourning. Instead, she carried on with her sadness bottled up within. She did start leaving work a little earlier in the day, but that was the only concession to grief that she would permit herself. When we are depressed, our resistance to illness is lowered, and our physical health deteriorates.

Mike Stermon suffered his first heart attack at the end of 1983. For Mother, family was always most important. While business was her life, it would have meant little without her family. Kathy had taken a business trip to Chicago and was staying with Larry, when the hospital called with the news. Mike's heart had stopped twice and each time had to be restarted with the defibrillator paddles. Mother spent the night at the hospital to make sure he knew she was there for him, and waiting for Kathy to arrive back to Houston. Mother was so worried about Mike, and by association her son Larry, she could hardly stand up to walk out of the hospital. Worry would take the form of pain in her back and hips, to the point that she sometimes needed support when she walked. Mike did survive that heart attack, although he needed time to recuperate, and he needed to change his diet and ease the stress in his life.

Worry over her family did not slow Helen down as far as the *Greensheet* was concerned. She continued to work long hours every day. She filled her mind with the work of growing her business, putting her emotional life on hold or burying it altogether under hundreds of activities. This may be why her health began to deteriorate. The pain she experienced in her back and hips must have been her body's way of telling her that she needed to take a break and let herself heal.

Mike Stermon died in March 1986. Both young men had survived the Vietnam War and returned home essentially intact to start families of their own, only to die of heart attacks years later.

In the midst of her grief over the loss of her son, it became obvious that one of Dan's boys could not take care of his son. Justin was then three years old and being shunted from one household to another. Helen volunteered to help Uncle Dan and take care of Justin on weekends. Uncle Dan took care of him during the week while he was at school. At work, Helen kept the worst of her grief over the loss of her son at bay by diving into work and refusing to participate in any conversation that would bring her emotions to the surface.

In some respects, Kathy followed her example after the death of her husband, but she soon realized it would be easier to move out of the house where they had lived and away from those places they had shared. She asked Helen if there was a city she could move to, either to establish a new office for the *Greensheet* or to take over one that already existed.

Our San Antonio office had not been selling as many ads as we thought it should, so Helen sent her there. This was in the fall of 1986, and Kathy believed this move would be the challenge she needed so she would not have to think about her loss. For Kathy, immersing herself in work in order to deal with the pain of loss did help. Shortly after she established herself in San Antonio, Helen let the manager in Austin go, and Kathy took that office over as well.

No matter what sorts of problems the manager in Austin may have created, the people who worked there knew what they were doing to the extent that the office nearly ran itself. Kathy only had to be there once a week to oversee and implement the changes and expectations that Helen wanted established. This way she could spend more time in San Antonio, attempting to figure out why they were not able to sell as many ads as the other large cities did. We sent two of the best salesmen from the Dallas office down to San Antonio, Mike Dagel and Gary Huggins (Gary still works with the *Greensheet* in Dallas), expecting that they would be able to do as well there as they had in Dallas. To our surprise, they were not able to bring the volume of sales up in San Antonio, nor were they able to sell any of the more expensive ads. The economy there was not strong enough to support an ad sheet like the *Greensheet*. Kathy and Helen discussed the problem and tried a few different ways to bring in the money. Their first thought was to charge customers for the *Greensheet*. To this end, they started having it distributed in lock boxes on street corners. Sales plummeted. The next option they tried was delivering it to peoples' homes and businesses. This might have worked as sales started coming in, except they had already lost so much money when they charged for the *Greensheet* that it was more expedient to simply close that office. Kathy went back to Houston and more or less hung out for the next six months, uncertain of where she would go or what she would do.

Mother worked hard and well in order to grow her business. She did this not only for herself, although toward the end she did pay herself lavishly, and not simply for her family, though she did everything she could to make sure that all of us would be financially secure. She wanted to make a difference in the world. When she married Bob, she began to help take care of his family as well. In 1985, his son Brian moved to Houston with the young woman who would be his wife. I suspect she must still have been feeling emotionally taut and brittle, as she still would not talk about Larry, or even mention his name in casual conversation. Brian had just graduated from college and was looking for work in Houston, so he and Julie stayed with Bob and our mother for a few months until Brian could find a job and a place where they could live. Our mother welcomed the two of them into her home. Shortly after they arrived, Julie expressed an interest in learning how to play the piano. Mother gave her lessons while they were there, and once they were ready to move into an apartment of their own, Mother bought them a piano so that Julie could continue to practice. Julie and Brian cherished that piano, taking it with them across the country when they moved. For Bob's son and daughter-in-law, the piano was an immense gift, but for Mother it was simply something nice to do. Brian remembers her saying, "I must have bought enough pianos in my life to fill a store."

Julie's mother had died when she was about nine years old. Mother, who had not so long before lost her son, felt drawn to Julie. In 1986, Julie and Brian decided to get married. She told Julie, "Let me be your mother" and proceeded to arrange a wedding that the two of them would always remember with fondness. I had become inured to Mother's extravagant productions and had long since learned to accept that this was the way she did things. However, for Bob's son and Julie, what she did was far more special than either of them expected.

Helen tried to keep the office in Chicago running for several years after Larry's death, believing that if it did well, it would be to her son's honor. The people who ran that office were not up to the task. Many businessmen in Chicago would rather barter for services or make deals than pay money. Occasionally this sort of business dealing works out well. However, you cannot run a business exclusively that way. Rent, paper, and employees all have to be paid with money. That office ultimately lost so much money, and Helen was so heartsick and disgusted every time she had to go out there, that she closed it.

Soon after its completion in 1987, Helen and Bob realized that their vacation house, now called Tamarack, in honor of that strong, beautiful tree, was too big to maintain on weekends, so the two of them moved in and spent a lot of money decorating and furnishing the place. It was built like a fine vacation hotel. There were four rooms on the first floor in back, near the garage entrance, specifically for live-in help. Guests were welcome to stay overnight, and they could do a variety of things, such as play pool in the basement poolroom, play a nine-hole round of golf, or go out on the pier to fish. If nothing else, they could enjoy the view. The house and grounds were spacious enough that she and Bob did not feel they had to constantly entertain their guests. My sister and I have wonderful memories of visiting with our mother there, and I am certain Bob got a real kick out of being grandfather to all our children.

Mother's dream had been to make it be a place where all our families—Kathy's, Larry's, Dan's, and mine—could get together for holidays, celebrations, and reunions and where she could invite her friends to relax in whatever ways they chose. Larry and Mike had already died by the time that house was built, and although our families did get together there for every holiday and for family reunions, she never did have the enthusiasm to do the sort of entertaining she once would have liked.

In 1990, Brian's wife, Julie, came down with what turned out to be multiple sclerosis. With this illness, the protective myelin sheath along the efferent nerve tracts, those tracts controlling movement, is steadily destroyed, making it more and more difficult for the patient to move in a coordinated fashion. There are drugs that can be given to slow down the progress of this disease, and most doctors agree that a diet high in omega-3s can be helpful, although there is little that can be done to check the progress of the disease.

Mother flew Julie back to Houston so that she could consult with the best MS specialist possible. Not only that, but she paid for Julie's healthcare so that she could have the best of the available treatments. Julie and Brian considered everything Mother did to be a godsend. Mother felt she was only doing what she should do, being a decent human being and helping people when she was able to do so. I believe that one of her basic reasons for working so hard to build up her business was so she could help the people she knew in tangible ways that would make a difference in their lives.

As the years went by and Mother was able to live more luxuriously, she developed a reputation for being generous. Even plumbers and electricians hired to do work in her home would approach her with their hands out. Many people who have money have experienced this problem, and many deal with it by closing themselves off and becoming fearful and angry that there is always someone else who wants or needs money. Perhaps there is no perfect way to deal with this situation. Helen did what she believed was best, making certain that all the members of her family were well taken care of and that at least some other people would have a chance to lead dignified lives, giving them the sort of chance that society likely would not. I'm thinking of the women she helped whose husbands had been abusing them. While Helen was a Republican in terms of the way she ran her business, she was a Democrat in the way she dealt with individuals. After all, she knew what it is like to have to do without material things, and she knew what it is like to have to scratch for a living.

Retiring Is Like Losing Your Watch

THE 1990S WAS ANOTHER DIFFICULT decade for Helen. She adopted her great nephew Justin in the midnineties. Justin went to live with Mother and Bob in 1991, and Helen adopted him in 1994. Thereafter she always claimed him as her son. Helen was in her sixties, and not feeling as though she should have to be a parent again. Still, he definitely needed someone who would be constant in his life. He had been shunted from one caretaker to another through his early childhood, and he was understandably angry at the entire world, not the easiest child to take care of. Helen did the best she could for him. Helen believed the family and taking care of the family was most important in her life. She said, "Life is a composite of those things that are near and dear, and people in the family, of course, are first and foremost. They comprise the basis that makes life worth living, and that includes the children."

Several years after Justin came to live at Tamarack, her granddaughter Laura, Larry's daughter, turned sixteen. Laura and her mother were having such intense battles that she and her brother Lawrence decided it would be nicer to live with their grandmother at Tamarack. Laura was going to a boarding school at the time, so for the most part, she was only with Helen on weekends and over the holidays. Lawrence was in college and very seldom came back home. It wasn't easy for Helen to deal with the three children. She no longer had the complete freedom to relax and do as she pleased. One time, Helen and Bob were going out to celebrate New Year's Eve. Laura asked if she could have a few friends over, and Helen told her she could. Lawrence was at home on vacation and he decided he would have a few of his friends over as well. It turned out to be too many young people, with a housekeeper unable to control the activities. Helen decided it would be best if she and Bob did not go out for New Year's Eve again, as long as Laura and Lawrence were at Tamarack.

For over twenty years, work had been Mother's major drive. She had poured her soul into the *Greensheet*. Nearly every thought and every action was directed toward building her business. Larry was gone and Kathy and I were competent young businesswomen. We were both smart and capable, though we did not always see eye to eye with Helen where running the *Greensheet* was concerned.

My first husband and I had divorced. I would call it an amicable divorce, as we are still friendly. I was still working full-time for the *Greensheet*, which meant that I was away from home a lot more than I was there. Therefore, I hired a nanny to be with my children. No matter how wonderful the nanny may be, there is a period of adjustment, as both the parents and the children need to get used to her being there. I was lucky, in that the woman I hired was a gem. Still, as with any growing family, a tremendous amount happened at home that I only heard about second- or thirdhand. I longed to be there.

I knew how to run a *Greensheet* office and make sure it ran smoothly. I had been working for the *Greensheet* for twenty-two years, and while I enjoyed my work and I was proud of what I have accomplished, there were times when the pressure of juggling home and work life had been too much. I do recall complaining to my mother, when I was dashing off to meet a flight to attend a meeting of one sort or another. I was saying disconnected things about just about everything. Mother understood that I was having an anxiety attack. She knew I was dealing with a lot of stress in my home life. She was also concerned for my health. Both Larry and Mike had died of heart conditions that had been augmented by their high-pressure positions. She did not want that happening to either of her daughters. She sat me down in her office one day and asked me point-blank, "If you could continue drawing pay, would you work for the *Greensheet* or would you be at home with your children?" I said that I would be with my children.

There have been times, many times, that I have missed the sense of responsibility and the sense of accomplishment that I always had working for the *Greensheet*. However, it had never been a part-time job, and during those years when my children were young, part-time work would have been much more reasonable for me. However, you cannot run a *Greensheet* office part-time.

It wasn't long after I left the *Greensheet* that Helen dropped into my sister's office to say, "Are you ready to run the *Greensheet*?" Kathy was a little bit stunned. She remembers saying, "Well, yes. Tell me what this means?"

"It's easy," Helen said. "All you have to do is write up your five-year plan, put it in a drawer, and know that it will happen."

This seemed simplistic to Kathy. "I want to share the plan with others, not put it in a drawer."

Helen was sixty-four at the time. It may have been early to retire, but she had earned it, if she could only learn how to enjoy doing other things that were not centered on the *Greensheet*. One of the reasons she stepped down when she did was so she could see whether Kathy could really manage it well. If Kathy showed any sign of floundering, Helen expected she would be able to take it over again, until she could find someone else to fill her shoes.

Prior to all this, in 1990, Helen thought she would try another business. She started Gordon's Flowers, making bouquets of flowers that were freeze-dried, and then dipped in a plastic solution to preserve them. This business combined her love of growing a variety of roses and business. Helen had expected to run this business during her retirement years, and then perhaps another member of her family would be able to take it over. The machinery for this was expensive, although she did buy ten of those freeze dryers and set them up on the second floor of our Main Street building. She also hired eight people to work with her there. She owned more freeze dryers than any other such operation in this country. Helen had a variety of rosebushes growing at Tamarack, which would reap at least 1,500 rose heads a week. She used the blooms and petals from these to make freeze-dried flower arrangements. She also preserved wedding bouquets and other flower arrangements for her customers. The flowers are arranged in the drier, where they spend eighteen days going through the freeze-drying process. When they come out, they are treated with a form of plastic to help preserve them. Producing beautiful freeze-dried flowers is not a quick-and-easy process. They must be gently handled throughout, until the final step, and even then they must be protected from paper mites. This was a vastly different sort of operation from establishing and running the *Greensheet*, which Helen understood and loved so well. It was an operation suited to the kind of person who likes to take his time to produce beautiful things and for whom money is a secondary concern. That never had been Helen's way.

Michelle Stermon, Kathy's daughter, started working for Helen in the first stages of this business. She was living in San Antonio with her husband and daughter, Cora, and Helen convinced Michelle a move to Houston to help her in her new venture would be a positive move for her family. Michelle learned the business, sold the product to customers, designed arrangements, and came up with new ideas on how to sell the freeze-dried products. Michelle learned every aspect of the business. Helen was a taskmaster, but Michelle survived and managed well with Helen. After about three years of working with Helen, Michelle and her family decided to move back to San Antonio.

Mother eventually found the work with flowers to be dull, not requiring the activity she was used to with the *Greensheet*. She now had too much time on her hands. She would spend some time with Kathy during the day to keep up with what was happening with the *Greensheet*. She refrained, for the most part, from offering advice, unless Kathy asked for it. Kathy was making reasonable and thoughtful decisions and doing well. The *Greensheet* did go through a difficult time financially before Helen retired, but Kathy was taking it in stride. In some ways, she appeared to thrive on the pressure to do well. Years later, Kathy said of that time that she had to make sure the *Greensheet* ran well, because 350 families were depending on her success.

Then came *Greensheet's* twenty-fifth year anniversary party, in 1995. Kathy made a big celebration of that, inviting all the department and office heads and renting the banquet room of a large hotel. There Kathy presented Helen with a lovely book, a collection of letters, snippets, and stories written by the people she had worked with, describing a little of what it had been like for them to help build the *Greensheet* and their appreciation of Helen. She was deeply touched that so many people had taken the time to write such nice things about her. Still, it was an anniversary party. She had spent years of her life building up the *Greensheet* and nursing it along so that it would truly be a viable business, capable of competing with some of the corporate giants. She had been both midwife and mother to it. Before that, she had brought every ounce of her sagacity to learning and understanding the advertising businesses where she had worked. In addition, all her life preceding that, when Kathy, Larry, and I were little, had been an almost constant exploration of all the ways she could earn not only a decent living but also a good living.

She looked around and realized that she would not need to take over the business from Kathy. Kathy was doing an excellent job of growing into the leadership position. For Helen, she felt as though she were attending her own funeral. When I asked her about her feelings after retiring, she said that it was like losing her watch. Where are all the people, where are the buildings? A feeling of loss. The lovely book of memories Kathy had put together for her, along with so many of the people who had worked with her, was filled with the sorts of things one would say at a memorial service. While Helen had been staying abreast of what was going on, she really was not in control of it anymore, and this celebration brought it home to her. After the anniversary party Helen and Bob traveled around the world in thirty days, via the Concord. When they returned, she came down with the worst case of shingles her doctor had ever seen. It took six months for the sores to heal and for the pain to go down enough that she could begin to function again.

Shingles manifests as patches of blisters on the skin that look like as though they were caused by burns. It is caused by the *Varicella zoster* virus—the same virus that causes chicken pox in children. Chicken pox was one of those childhood illnesses that everyone had when Helen was a little girl. Once the chicken pox are healed, the virus lies dormant along our sensory nerve tracts, usually waiting many years, for a time when our immune system is under stress, and then it flares up as shingles. The death of a loved one, the loss of a job, or any other great change in life can trigger the virus to reactivate. Regular deep breathing and meditative exercises performed outside in the sunshine do help prevent it. Up until then, Helen had been too busy working to think about spending time outside relaxing. Work had been her life. She kept her nerves calm by smoking cigarettes. Added to this, her home life with Justin and Laura was very demanding. Her case of shingles was so painful that she had to remain in bed for several weeks, and she lost a lot of weight during that time. How much Helen's depression over letting go of the *Greensheet* had to do with her getting sick is hard to say. Gordon Flowers had never been enough to hold her interest. She was done with the flower business; therefore, it was time to pass it on to someone else to manage. It was Gordon Flowers that brought my family and me back to Houston in 1997. The best part of running Gordon Flowers was working with Helen again. She ran the rose garden in La Porte while I was in charge of the machines, production, and marketing. We kept the business until in 2004, when it became obvious to everyone involved that there was no way we could keep it from losing money.

On one of her trips to the doctor to get pain medication for her shingles, the doctor discovered she had no circulation in her legs. He told her to go to the hospital immediately. He said that if she went home to collect her things, she would have to go to the hospital in an ambulance. His staff settled Helen into a wheelchair and took her directly to the hospital.

That was when Mother stopped smoking. Kathy recalls Mother saying, during what may have been the last time she lit up a cigarette, "I can feel my veins tightening up when I do this." Smoking does constrict the arterial blood flow, slowing down circulation to the heart and lungs. A classic way to stimulate a heart attack is to stand outside when the snow is about two feet deep, light up a cigarette, and start shoveling the snow. That combination of cold, hard exercise, and the effect tobacco smoke has on coronary arteries puts a tremendous amount of stress on the heart and the circulatory system. Many people have been carted off to the hospital, suffering from a major heart attack after doing just those things, in that order.

Most habitual smokers find that it takes a lot of will power to stop smoking. I look back and wish that Mother had been able to stop years before she did. When she did at last stop, she gained a lot of weight. The lack of activity, coupled with the medications she took to ease the pain and inflammation, and the weight started to pile on. A pound here and a pound there do add up very quickly. Many people claim that, at least for those first few months after they stop smoking, they find themselves substituting food for cigarettes. Mother had always liked rich food. It wasn't long before she realized she had gained more weight than she could handle, especially as the circulation to her legs was so badly compromised. She needed surgery to ease the blockage enough that she could walk again. She also needed multiple stents to her heart to increase the circulation there. It took several months for her to recover from all those surgeries.

Mother always loved to shop for fine things. She loved the way the salespeople would treat her when she walked into a store. They knew she had plenty of money to spend and that she wanted nothing but the best they had to offer. I recall walking into Neiman Marcus with my mother when she shopped for clothes and jewelry. She had been to those stores so often and spent so much money on fine clothing for her work and other fine luxuries that the salespeople would line up, ready to serve her, as soon as she appeared on their floor. They gave her the sort of respect generally reserved for visiting dignitaries. It was reminiscent of the opening scene in the television series *Upstairs, Downstairs,* with the servants lined up to pay their respects to the master as he alights from his carriage.

She had a personal shopper at Neiman Marcus, Randy Plante, who became a very good friend. I am not certain whose idea it had been originally, whether Mother's or Randy's. Mother was still quite sick and using a wheelchair to get around, but she thought it would be wonderful to fly to New York City with Randy and spend a week or so going to the shows and the stores and the restaurants Mother had always loved.

Bob was very worried. Mother's health had been too close to the edge for him. He had put his foot down not too long before over taking another trip to Europe. He did not want to run the risk of having to take Mother to a hospital in a foreign country, where many of the doctors did not speak English and none of them had the background information on Mother's health problems. For those same reasons, he wasn't at all happy about Mother's going to New York City.

Mother and Randy talked about this trip for quite a while before Bob at last said, "Okay. Go." The two of them went and had a delightful time. Randy was an excellent planner. She made sure there was always someone there to help guide Mother's wheelchair through crowds and to elevators. She made sure they had a good, workable plan in case worse came to worst and Mother needed immediate medical attention.

As far as Mother was concerned, the trip was, in every sense of the word, a success. The two of them talked about it with fondness for months afterward. When she returned to Tamarack, she decided it was definitely time for her to learn how to get along without the wheelchair. Gradually, Bob began to take her for walks around the perimeter of their property. As the weeks went by, she discovered that swimming was very helpful, and for a couple of months she hired a navy seal to coach her while she swam, until she reached the point where she felt she really didn't need that sort of coaching any more.

It was in 2004 that Helen and Bob came to the realization that Tamarack was a tremendous expense and that it would be a good idea for her to move back to Houston, where she would be closer to the hospitals. Helen loved going back to the city, as she felt much less isolated there than she had at Tamarack. There were plenty of stores and restaurants that she always enjoyed going to, as she was treated so well whenever she went.

The move was harder for Bob. He was depressed over no longer having the garage space he had enjoyed at Tamarack for his collection of cars. When they moved back to Houston, he had to get rid of some of his favorite cars, and he had to find another space to store the ones that were left, a space that was farther away from their home and did not give him that pleasant feeling of ownership that he had enjoyed at Tamarack.

Swimming became very important to Mother after she moved to Houston. She discovered that when she swam every day, her blood pressure stayed at a normal level, but when she did not, it went up and she had to take medications to keep it down.

In 1993, Mother decided she would take up painting again. She liked painting portraits, as she had had some good experiences painting portraits of children when we were little. This time, she wanted to do paintings of well-known people whom she respected. She did not want to charge for her work, as she believed that if she did, she would have to paint portraits of anyone who came to her with money in hand. She hired a publicist to let it be known that she would paint portraits of well-known, respected individuals for free. All that Helen asked was some time with the individual to meet them, interview them, and take a few photographs. Helen specifically wanted to paint people who had accomplished something in life and had charismatic personalities.

When you offer something as personal as a portrait, you need to know what the person wants to look like in the finished product. Children tend to look adorable no matter how you pose them. Adults, however, often have defects they would like to pretend are not there. There was one fellow who was not at all happy that the portrait she painted for him, which actually looked like him. Someone else was upset over the fact that she had painted his nose as it appeared in his photographs. He had wanted a smaller one. However, she did paint portraits for Dr. Debakey, Dave Ward, Carloyn Farb, M. Hallbuty, Racehorse Haines, John Maddon, Dr. Rev. Morledge, Leo Womack, Leo Kissner, Tony Vallone, James Baker, President George Bush Sr., Dr. Choo, and of course Bob De Young. She never enjoyed anyone criticizing her work, and that was why she did not get the enjoyment out of portrait painting that she had thought she might. She had been painting portraits almost since she was a child. Of course, she could create remarkable likenesses of people; it was simply that people did not always want to have a remarkable likeness of themselves.

Mother continued to play the piano, practicing difficult pieces at least two hours every day. Mother also decided learn to play the harp. She bought a six-foot harp, which she played until she no longer had the strength to tune it. She had always seen creating beautiful music as a challenge to be mastered, and Mother always liked meeting challenges. Even as a child, when her instructor told her to learn one piece in her book, Helen would learn that one and then work on a much more difficult piece. People did not tend to criticize her playing.

Up until the day she was diagnosed with cancer in October 2009, Helen had plans to do more things, perhaps by a business and act as director to ensure that it would grow. She had been very successful with the *Greensheet*, as advertising was something she understood and enjoyed. Good advertising along with developing a reputable name is the soul of nearly every business. Helen had spent twenty-five years of her life building up a business, based entirely on advertising that was enviably successful.

Above all else, Helen was an example to everyone who knew her of what it can mean to be an independent woman. She came out of an era when women were routinely told not to worry about money. Ladies were better off keeping their hands off it. Even now, when women entrepreneurs sit down with their clients, it is difficult for them to talk about money, or even to admit that they need to be paid for the work they do. Helen, of course, would have none of that. My sister, brother, and I grew up to understand the value of money and how to work for it. She taught my sister and I that we could and should be ladies and that being ladies would not at all detract from our being good businesspeople.

Helen was an example for all the people who worked for her, although it may be difficult to clarify what sort of example she was.

She was a complicated and unique woman who enjoyed drama and who liked seeing the people who worked for her actively compete with each other. Those who worked well with her, even some of those who could not manage to work well in her office, claim they learned a tremendous amount from observing how she conducted her business. Kathy and I learned the sort of energy and dedication it takes to make a business work and the ability to not be afraid to make choices. Yes, money does open doors, and we are all very grateful for the fact that we have that money. Above and beyond the choices that money makes possible, Helen taught us not to be afraid of making choices and decisions on our own. She taught us not to be ashamed to speak up for ourselves. Yes, we should always speak up in a ladylike manner, but we should speak up nonetheless and be true to what we believe is right.

We learned from our mother the value of family. In an age when siblings may live thousands of miles away and never see each other, she taught us that it is good for the psyche and good for the soul to keep those connections strong. More than that, she taught us that it is our duty to do what we can to make sure the members of our family have what they need, and to help them live comfortably.

In one of the last interviews I had with my mother, I asked her about when she had first felt she was successful. She turned that conversation around very quickly, saying that being successful means you are superb at any number of things. "I wouldn't call myself a successful painter or a successful pianist." I had to bring the conversation back to her experience running the *Greensheet*. I pointed out the milestones she had achieved when she ran that paper—buying her first car, buying expensive clothes to wear at her office, paying herself a reasonable salary. None of those things had made her feel successful because, as she put it, "there was always another mountain to climb."

It has become obvious to me that Mother was driven to live her life on a grand scale. Perhaps she always had been. She was determined not only to maintain control of her life but to do all those things that most of us only dream about—see plays on Broadway, travel to exotic places, go out to fine restaurants whenever she chose, and live in a large, comfortable house where she could entertain her family and a few close friends. Ultimately, she was able to choose how she should be taken care of when she was no longer able to take care of herself.

Mother died of lung cancer on March 31, 2010, the end of the *Greensheet's* fiscal year. We knew she was ill, although I don't believe any of us suspected she was so close to dying. I had been interviewing her for this book during the summer of 2009. She was eighty years old. She was excited about the book, but her voice was husky from years of smoking and she frequently had to stop talking in order to cough. The cough was from the cancer, but we did not know that at the time. Even so, she saw life as a banquet, filled with things she believed she could do and would do. She had been talking with her bankers and financial advisors about buying another small business and helping it grow. Guiding the growth of the *Greensheet* had been exhilarating, and she wanted to repeat that experience as much as her energy would permit. Putting people to work in a fast-paced business, telling them what to do, and seeing that the decisions she made were profitable—that was where the excitement had been. Intellectually she knew she should slow down, but emotionally she would have loved to get back into the driver's seat of a small business, seeing her ideas build into something powerful. She could never bring herself to believe that this illness would be her final one.

Epilogue

IN 2013, THE *GREENSHEET* CELEBRATES forty-three years of successful business, which all started from Helen Gordon's initial intent to own her own business. Kathy's vision is to take it to one hundred years. Helen started with one edition in southwest Houston, with a circulation of 20,000 papers. The *Greensheet* now prints twenty editions in Texas and is online. With twelve editions in Houston, four in Dallas, three in Fort Worth, and one in Austin, there is now a total verified pickup of 660,000 papers each week.

Decades of building the successful business that *Greensheet* is today has involved the commitment of everyone who has ever worked at the *Greensheet*. The belief that training associates is a high priority—developing a culture and environment within the company of strong work ethics and values—is what drives the *Greensheet* and all the associates. Drawing its strength from the associates who work there and a family commitment to success, the *Greensheet* will continue to expand each service it provides, carrying the company to 2070 and beyond.